THE BASIC ESSENTIALS OF ISLAM

المَبادِئ الأسَاسِيَّة لِلإسْلام

BY

Dr. Abdossalam Salem Aboasha

د. عبدالسّلام سالم أبوعيشه

The Basic Essentials of Islam

First Edition: 2019 – 1441

Revised Edition: 2023 – 1444

Printed in the United States of America

Library of Congress Control Number: 2019904871

ISBN-13: 978-0-578-47632-2

المَبادِئ الأسَاسِيَّة لِلإسْلام

د. عبدالسّلام سالم أبو عيشه

Email: aa.aboasha@gmail.com

الآيَات وَالسّور فِي هَذا الكِتَاب مَكتُوبَة
بِرِوَايَة حَفْصٍ عَن عَاصِم

بِسْمِ اللَّهِ الرَّحْمَـٰنِ الرَّحِيمِ

In the Name of Allah, the Most Gracious, the Most Merciful

﴿إِنَّ الدِّينَ عِنْدَ اللَّهِ الْإِسْلَامُ﴾

[آلِ عِمْرَان: 91]

"Surely the religion with Allah is Islam"

[3: 19]

Book Contents (1) مُحتويات الكِتاب

(1) For more details see Index page 153 لِمزيد مِن التَّفاصيل انظر الفهرس صفحة 153

Dedication الإهْدَاء

أُهْدِي كِتَابِي هَذا لِوَالِدَيَّ اللَّذَيْنِ قَامَا بِتَرْبِيَتِي، وحَرِصَا عَلَى تَعْلِيمِي وَصَبرَا عَلَى غُرْبَتِي، فَأسْأَلُ اللهَ الْعَظِيمَ بِأسْمَائِهِ الْحُسْنَى وَصِفاتِهِ الْعُلَا أَنْ يَرْحَمَهُمَا وَيُدخِلَهُمَا الْجَنَّة.

(رَبِّ ارْحَمْهُمَا كَمَا رَبَّيَانِي صَغِيرًا)

I dedicate my book to my parents, who raised me, educated me, and they were patient while I was away from them. I ask Allah Almighty by His Beautiful Names and His High Attributes to bless them and to accept them in His Paradise.

"My Lord! Have Your Mercy upon them, as they raised me when I was young."

Acknowledgments شُكْر وَتقْدِير

أحْمَدُ اللهَ، عَزَّ وَجَلَّ، الّذِي وَفَّقَنِي لإتْمَامِ هَذَا الْكِتَابِ، وأشْكُرُهُ عَلى نِعَمِهِ الْكَثِيرَةِ الّتِي لَا تُحْصَى، وَبَعْد:

أتَوَجَّهُ بِالشُّكْرِ لِكُلّ عَائِلَتِي لِمُساعدتِهم وتَشْجِيعِهم الْغَيْرِ مَحْدُود أثْنَاء إعْدَادِ هَذا الكِتَاب.

وَأَيْضًا أوَدُّ أنْ أشْكُرَ إبْنِي ضِيَاءَ، وإبْنَتِي أسْمَاءَ لِقِرَاءتِهما لِلنُّسْخَةِ الْأولَى مِنْ هَذَا الْكِتاب، وَلإقْتِراحَاتِهمَا الْقَيِّمَةِ فِيمَا يَخُصُّ قِسْم اللّغَة الْإنْجلِيزِيّة.

كَمَا أتَوَجَّهُ بِالشُّكْرِ لِجَمِيعِ الْأصْدِقاء الّذِينَ قَدَّمُوا لِي مُلَاحظَاتِهِمْ وَاقْتِرَاحَاتِهِمْ، وَإِلَى الَّذِينَ قَرَؤُوا كِتَابِيَ الْأوّل- **السَّبْعُونَ الْمُخْتَارَةُ مِنَ الصّحِيحَيْن** - وَشَجَّعُونِي عَلى الْإسْتِمْرَارِ فِي الْكِتابَةِ.

I praise Allah, the Almighty, Who has helped me to complete this book, and I thank Him for His countless graces.

With sincere appreciation, I would like to thank all of my family members for their continuous help, encouragement, and support during the preparation of this book.

I would also like to extend a special thanks to my son, Dyia, and my daughter, Asmaa, for taking the time to read the first draft of this book and for their valuable suggestions of the English section.

Finally, I would like to thank my friends who shared their suggestions and comments, and to those who read my first book- ***Seventy Selected Hadith From Al-Bukhari and Muslim****- and encouraged me to continue writing.*

بِسْمِ اللهِ الرَّحْمَـٰنِ الرَّحِيمِ

إنَّ الْحَمْدَ للهِ، نَحْمَدُهُ وَنَسْتَعِينُهُ وَنَسْتَغْفِرُهُ، وَنَعُوذُ بِاللهِ مِنْ شُرُورِ أَنْفُسِنَا وَمِنْ سَيِّئَاتِ أَعْمَالِنَا، مَنْ يَهْدِهِ اللهُ فَلا مُضِلَّ لَهُ، وَمَنْ يُضْلِلْ فَلا هَادِيَ لَهُ، وَأَشْهَدُ أَنْ لَا إِلَـهَ إِلَّا اللهُ وَحْدَهُ لَا شَرِيكَ لَهُ، وَأَشْهَدُ أَنَّ مُحَمَّدًا عَبْدُهُ وَرَسُولُهُ.

﴿يَا أَيُّهَا الَّذِينَ آمَنُوا اتَّقُوا اللهَ حَقَّ تُقَاتِهِ وَلَا تَمُوتُنَّ إِلَّا وَأَنتُم مُّسْلِمُونَ﴾ [آلِ عِمْرَان: 102].

﴿يَا أَيُّهَا النَّاسُ اتَّقُوا رَبَّكُمُ الَّذِي خَلَقَكُمْ مِنْ نَفْسٍ وَاحِدَةٍ وَخَلَقَ مِنْهَا زَوْجَهَا وَبَثَّ مِنْهُمَا رِجَالًا كَثِيرًا وَنِسَاءً وَاتَّقُوا اللهَ الَّذِي تَسَاءَلُونَ بِهِ وَالأَرْحَامَ إِنَّ اللهَ كَانَ عَلَيْكُمْ رَقِيبًا﴾ [النِّسَاء: 1].

﴿يَا أَيُّهَا الَّذِينَ آمَنُوا اتَّقُوا اللهَ وَقُولُوا قَوْلًا سَدِيدًا • يُصْلِحْ لَكُمْ أَعْمَالَكُمْ وَيَغْفِرْ لَكُمْ ذُنُوبَكُمْ وَمَن يُطِعِ اللهَ وَرَسُولَهُ فَقَدْ فَازَ فَوْزًا عَظِيمًا﴾ [الأحْزَاب: 70 – 71].

أَمَّا بَعْد: فَهَذَا الْكِتَاب يَتَنَاوَلُ الْمَبادِئ الأسَاسِيَّةَ لِلإسْلامِ – الَّتِي يَحْتَاجُهَا الْمُسْلِم – بِطَرِيقَةٍ سَهْلَةٍ مُبسَّطَةٍ لِطَلَبَةِ الْمَدَارِسِ، وَلِمَنْ لَهُ الرَّغْبَةُ فِي التَّعرُّفِ عَلَى الإسْلامِ.

لَقَد تَحَرَّيْتُ الدِّقَةَ مَا اسْتَطَعْتُ لِذلِك سَبِيلًا، وَإِنْ وُجِدَت بَعْضَ الأَخْطَاءِ فَأَرْجُو مِنَ الْجَمِيعِ تَنْبِيهي لِذَلِك، وَلَكُم جَزِيلُ الشُّكْرِ.

أَسْأَلُ اللهَ الْعَظِيمَ أَنْ يَجْعَلَ هَذَا الْعَمَلَ خَالِصًا لَهُ، وَأَنْ يَجْعَلَ لَهُ الْقَبُول وَيَنْفَعَ بِهِ، وَآخِرُ دَعْوَانَا أَنِ الْحَمْدُ للهِ رَبِّ الْعَالَمِين، وَالصَّلاةُ وَالسَّلامُ عَلَى نَبِيِّنَا مُحَمَّدٍ وَعَلَى آلِهِ وَصَحْبِهِ أَجْمَعِين.

د . عبدالسّلام سالم أبو عيشه 1441/2 هـ - 2019/10 م

In the Name of Allah, the Most Gracious, the Most Merciful

All praise be to Allah the Almighty. We praise Him, seek His help, and ask for His forgiveness. We seek refuge with Allah from the evil within ourselves and our sinful deeds. He, whom Allah guides, no one can mislead him and he whom He misguides, no one can guide. And I bear witness that there is no deity worthy of worship except Allah. And I bear witness that Muhammad is His servant and Messenger.

"*O you who believe! Fear Allah as He should be feared, and die not unless you are Muslims.*" [2: 102].

"O mankind! Fear your Lord, Who created you from one soul and created from it its mate and dispersed from both of them many men and women. And fear Allah, through Whom you ask one another, and the wombs. Indeed Allah is ever, over you, an Observer." [4: 1].

"O you who believe! Guard your duty to Allah and fear Him, and speak the truth. He will direct you to do good deeds and will forgive your sins. And whoever obeys Allah and His Messenger, he has won a great victory." [33: 70-71].

To proceed:

This book is an introduction to the basic principles of Islam. It is for students and all those who desire to learn Islam.
To the best of my ability, I have made this work complete and accurate. If an error is found, would you please let me know and I would appreciate your comments or suggestions. I ask Allah Almighty to make this work sincere for His sake and to benefit from it. And our last request will be: All Praise be to Allah, Lord of the Worlds, and peace be upon our Prophet Muhammad, his household, and his companions.

Dr. Abdossalam Salem Aboasha ***10/2019 – 2/1441 AH***

العَقِيدَةُ الإسْلامِيَّةُ

The Islamic Creed

قَالَ اللهُ تَعَالَى:

﴿قُلْ إِنَّمَآ أَدْعُواْ رَبِّى وَلَآ أُشْرِكُ بِهِۦٓ أَحَدًا﴾

"Say, (O Muhammad), I call on my Lord alone, and I do not associate anyone with Him."

[72: 20] [الجِنّ: 20]

اِعْلَم - رَحِمَكَ اللهُ -

أَنَّ الإِخْلَاصَ شَرْط فِي كُلِّ العِبَادَات

Know, may God have mercy on you, that sincerity is a condition in all acts of worship

Islamic Creed – العَقِيدَةُ الإِسْلامِيَّةُ

الْعَقِيدَةُ الإِسْلَامِيَّةُ هِيَ الإِيمَانُ الْجَازِمُ بِكُلِّ مَا وَرَدَ فِي الْقُرْآنِ الْكَرِيمِ، وَالسُّنَّةِ الثَّابِتَةِ لِرَسُولِ اللهِ، ﷺ. فَالْعَقِيدَةُ الإِسْلامِيَّةُ تَشْمَلُ: الإِيمَانَ الْجَازِمَ بِوُجُودِ اللهِ، وَبِأَنَّهُ إِلَـهٌ وَاحِدٌ لَا شَرِيكَ لَهُ فِي رُبُوبِيَّتِهِ، وَأُلُوهِيَّتِهِ، وَأَسْمَائِهِ الْحُسْنَى وَصِفَاتِهِ الْعُلَا. وَمِنْ أُصُولِ الْعَقِيدَةِ الإِسْلامِيَّةِ الإِيمَانُ بِأَرْكَانِ الإِيمَانِ السِّتَّةِ، وَالإِيمَانُ وَالْعَمَلُ بِأَرْكَانِ الإِسْلامِ الْخَمْسَةِ، وَاعْلَم أَنَّ الشِّرْكَ يُحْبِطُ الْعَمَلَ.

قَالَ تَعَالَى: ﴿وَإِلَٰهُكُمْ إِلَٰهٌ وَاحِدٌ ۖ لَّا إِلَـهَ إِلَّا هُوَ الرَّحْمَٰنُ الرَّحِيمُ﴾ [البَقَرة: 163]. وَقَالَ تَعَالَى: ﴿هُوَ اللهُ الْخَالِقُ الْبَارِئُ الْمُصَوِّرُ ۖ لَهُ الْأَسْمَاءُ الْحُسْنَىٰ﴾ [الحَشر: 24].

وَقَالَ تَعَالَى: ﴿وَاعْبُدُوا اللهَ وَلَا تُشْرِكُوا بِهِ شَيْئًا﴾ [النِّساء: 36]. وَقَالَ تَعَالَى: ﴿وَلَوْ أَشْرَكُوا لَحَبِطَ عَنْهُم مَّا كَانُوا يَعْمَلُونَ﴾ [الأنْعام: 88].

وَقَالَ ﷺ: ((حَقُّ اللهِ عَلَى الْعِبَادِ أَنْ يَعْبُدُوهُ، وَلَا يُشْرِكُوا بِهِ شَيْئًا)) [البُخاري وَمُسْلِم].

The Islamic Creed is the firm belief in all that is contained in the Holy Qur'an and the authentic Sunnah of the Messenger of Allah; peace be upon him. The Islamic Creed encompasses the firm belief in the existence of Allah, the Oneness of Lordship, the Oneness of Worship, and the Oneness of Allah's Names and Attributes. Of the principles of the Islamic Creed is to believe in the six pillars of faith and to believe and perform the five pillars of Islam, and be aware that associating partners with Allah will invalidate good deeds. Allah said:

"And your Lord is One! There is no god but He, the Most Gracious, the Most Merciful." [2: 163]. Also, Allah said: "Worship Allah and associate nothing with Him." [4: 36]. In another verse, Allah said: "He is Allah, the Creator, the Originator, the Shaper Who shapes, all forms and appearances!" [59: 24]. And In another verse, Allah said: "If they had associated others with Allah, then all their deeds would have gone in vain (not accepted)." [6: 88].
In the Sunnah, the Prophet, peace be upon him, said: "The right of Allah is for worshipers to worship Him alone and not to associate Him with anything." [Al-Bukhari and Muslim].

Islamic Monotheism – التَّوْحِيد

أسَاسُ الْعَقِيدَةِ الْإسْلَامِيَّةِ التَّوْحِيدُ، وأسَاسُ التَّوْحِيدِ، **شَهَادَةُ أنْ لَا إلَـٰهَ إلَّا اللهُ وَأنَّ مُحَمّدًا رَسُولُ اللهِ**. هَذِهِ الشَّهَادَةُ لَابُدَّ مِنْ مَعْرِفَةِ مَعْنَاهَا، وَالْعَمَلِ بِمُقْتَضَاهَا، وَالدَّعْوَةِ إلَيْهَا. **شَهَادَةُ أنْ لَا إلَـٰهَ إلَّا اللهُ:** مَعْنَاهَا الْإقْرَارُ الْجَازِمُ بِالْقَلْبِ وَاللِّسَانِ بِأنَّهُ لَا مَعْبودَ بِحَقٍّ إلَّا الله وَحْدَهُ لَا شَرِيك لَهُ، وَأَنْ لَا يُعْبَدُ إلَّا بِمَا شَرَع. قَالَ اللهُ تَعَالَى: ﴿ شَهِدَ اللهُ أَنَّهُ لَا إلَـٰهَ إلَّا هُوَ وَالْمَلَائِكَةُ وَأُولُو الْعِلْمِ قَائِمًا بِالْقِسْطِ ۚ لَا إلَـٰهَ إلَّا هُوَ الْعَزِيزُ الْحَكِيمُ﴾ [آلِ عِمْرَان: 18].

The basis of the Islamic Creed is Tawheed (monotheism). And the basis of monotheism is the testimony that there is no god but Allah and that Muhammad is the Messenger of Allah. This testimony must be known and acted upon its meaning and advocate it. **The testimony that "there is no true god but Allah.":** means a firm acknowledgment that there is none has the right to be worshiped but Allah and He Who Has no partner. Allah Almighty said: "Allah bears witness that there is no god but He. The angels and those of knowledge also testified that there is no god but Him, the Exalted, the All-Wise." [3: 18].

وَشَهَادَةُ أَنَّ مُحَمَّدًا رَسُولُ اللهِ: مَعْنَاهَا الإِقْرَارُ وَالإِيمَانُ بِأَنَّهُ، صلى الله عليه وسلم، رَسُولُ اللهِ وَخَاتَمُ النَّبِيِّينَ، لَا نَبِيَّ بَعْدَهُ، وَهَذَا يَقْتَضِي وُجُوبَ طَاعَتِهِ، وَتَصْدِيقِهِ، وَالْتِزَامِ سُنَّتِهِ، وَاتِّبَاعِ شَرِيعَتِهِ. قَالَ اللهُ تَعَالَى: ﴿مَنْ يُطِعِ الرَّسُولَ فَقَدْ أَطَاعَ اللهَ﴾ [النساء: 80]، وَقَالَ تَعَالَى: ﴿وَمَا آتَاكُمُ الرَّسُولُ فَخُذُوهُ وَمَا نَهَاكُمْ عَنْهُ فَانْتَهُوا﴾ [الحشر: 7].

And the testimony that Muhammad is the Messenger of Allah: It means believing that he, peace be upon him, is the Messenger of Allah and the Seal of the Prophets (no Prophets or Messengers will come after him, peace be upon him). The testimony requires obedience to his orders, acceptance of his message, commitment to his way, and adherence to his Sunnah. Allah said: "And who obeys the messenger, obeyed Allah." [4: 80]. And in another verse, Allah said: "And whatever the Messenger (Muhammad) has given you, take it; and whatever he has forbidden you, refrain from it. And fear Allah; indeed, Allah's punishment is severe." [59: 7].

Glad Tidings - بُشْرَى سَارَّة

قَالَ ﷺ:

((مَنْ مَاتَ وَهُوَ يَعْلَمُ أَنَّهُ لَا إِلَهَ إِلَّا اللهُ دَخَلَ الْجَنَّةَ))

[رَوَاهُ مُسْلِم]

"Whoever dies knowing there is no god has the right to be worshipped but Allah will enter Paradise." [Muslim].

Monotheism Types - أَقْسَامُ التَّوْحِيد

قَسَّمَ الْعُلَمَاءُ التَّوْحِيدَ إِلَى ثَلَاثَةِ أقْسَامٍ- لِغَرَضِ التَّوْضِيح- وَهِيَ:
تَوْحِيدُ الرُّبُوبِيَّةِ، وَتَوْحِيدُ الأُلُوهِيَّةِ، وَتَوْحِيدُ الأَسْمَاءِ وَالصِّفَاتِ.

The scholars divided monotheism (for clarification) into three types: Oneness of Lordship, Oneness of Worship, and Oneness of Allah's Names and Aattributes.

تَوْحِيدُ الرُّبُوبِيَّةِ
Oneness of Lordship

تَوْحِيدُ الرُّبُوبِيَّةِ هُوَ الإِيمَانُ بِوُجُودِ اللهِ، سُبْحَانَهُ وتَعَالَى، وَالْإِقْرَارُ وَالْإِعْتِقَادُ الجَازِمُ بِأَنَّ اللهَ وَحْدَهُ هُوَ رَبُّ كُلِّ شَيْءٍ وَمَلِيكُهُ، وَهُوَ الْخَالِقُ، والْمُحْيِي، وَالْمُمِيتُ، وَالرَّازِقُ، وَالنَّافِعُ وَالضَّارُ، وَأنَّهُ هُوَ وَحْدَهُ يَخْلُقُ مَا يَشَاءُ وَيَخْتَارُ، وَأَنَّهُ عَلَى كُلِّ شَيْءٍ قَدِير.
قَالَ تَعَالَى: ﴿ذَٰلِكُمُ اللهُ رَبُّكُمْ فَتَبَارَكَ اللهُ رَبُّ الْعَالَمِينَ﴾ [غافر: 64].
وَقَالَ تَعَالَى: ﴿هُوَ اللهُ الْخَالِقُ الْبَارِئُ الْمُصَوِّرُ﴾ [الحَشر: 24].
وَقَالَ تَعَالَى: ﴿إِنَّ اللهَ هُوَ الرَّزَّاقُ ذُو الْقُوَّةِ الْمَتِينُ﴾ [الذّاريات: 58].

Oneness of Lordship: It means to believe in the existence of Allah and He is one without a partner. And to believe firmly that Allah, is the Lord and Sovereign of all things. He is the Creator, the One Who gives sustenance, life, and death. He is the only One Who creates and chooses what He wants, and He has power over all things. Allah, the Exalted, said: "That is Allah, your Lord, blessed be Allah, the Lord of all worlds!" [40: 64]. "He is Allah, the Creator, the One Who forms (all shapes and appearances)." [59: 24]. And in another Allah said: "Indeed Allah is the All-Provider, Almighty with the strongest Power." [51: 58].

Oneness of Worship - تَوْحِيدُ الأُلُوهِيَّةِ

تَوْحِيدُ الأُلُوهِيَّةِ هُوَ إِفْرَادُ اللهِ بِكُلِّ أَنْوَاعِ العِبَادَةِ – القَوْلِيَّةِ والفِعْلِيَّةِ – مِثْلُ: الصَّلَاةِ، وَالزَّكَاةِ، وَالدُّعَاءِ، وَالتَّوَكُّلِ، وَالاِسْتِعَانَةِ، وَالنَّذْرِ، وَالذَّبْحِ، وَالخَوْفِ، وَالرَّجَاءِ، وَالعَمَلِ بِكُلِّ مَا دَلَّ عَلَيْهِ الكِتَابُ الكَرِيمُ، وَالسُّنَّةُ الصَّحِيحَةُ لِرَسُولِ اللهِ صلى الله عليه وسلم.

قَالَ تَعَالَى: ﴿وَمَا خَلَقْتُ ٱلْجِنَّ وَٱلْإِنسَ إِلَّا لِيَعْبُدُونِ﴾ [الذاريات: 56].

وَقَالَ تَعَالَى: ﴿إِنَّنِي أَنَا اللهُ لَا إِلَـٰهَ إِلَّا أَنَا فَاعْبُدْنِي وَأَقِمِ الصَّلَاةَ لِذِكْرِي﴾ [طه: 14]. وَقَالَ تَعَالَى: ﴿قُلْ إِنَّ صَلَاتِي وَنُسُكِي وَمَحْيَايَ وَمَمَاتِي لِلهِ رَبِّ العَالَمِينَ * لَا شَرِيكَ لَهُ وَبِذَٰلِكَ أُمِرْتُ وَأَنَا أَوَّلُ المُسْلِمِينَ﴾ [الأنعام: 162 – 163].

Oneness of Worship: Means all types of worship – verbal and nonverbal- should be to Allah alone, such as prayer, zakah, supplication, hope, help, appeal, slaughter, fear, and trust. All this is shown by the Nobel Qur'an and the authentic Sunnah of the Prophet Muhammed, peace be upon him.

Allah, the Exalted, said: **"**And I did not create the jinn and mankind except to worship Me (Alone)." [51: 56].

In another verse, Allah said: **"**Verily, I am Allah: and there is no god but I, so worship Me, and perform the prayer for My remembrance." [20: 14]. And in another verse, Allah said: "Say: Verily, my prayer, my sacrifice, my living, and my dying are all for Allah, the Lord of the worlds. He has no partner, this is what I have been commanded, and I am the first of the Muslims." [6: 162- 163].

تَوْحِيدُ الْأَسْمَاءِ وَالصِّفَاتِ
Oneness of Allah's Names and Attributes

أَسْمَاءُ اللهِ وَصِفَاتِهِ تَوْقِيفِيَّةٌ- أَيْ لَا سَبِيلَ لِلْإِجْتِهَادِ فِيهَا. فَعَلَى الْمُسْلِمِ الْإِيمَانُ والتَّصْدِيقُ بِكُلِّ مَا وَرَدَ فِي الْقُرْآنِ الْكَرِيمِ وَصَحّ فِي السُّنَّةِ النَّبوِيَّةِ مِنْ أسْمَاءِ اللهِ الْحُسْنَى وَصِفَاتِه الْعُلَا. أَيضًا يَجِبُ عَلَى الْمُسْلِمِ إِثْبَاتُ الْأَسْمَاءِ وَالصِّفَاتِ كَمَا وَرَدَت عَلى الْوَجْهِ اللَّائِقِ بِعَظَمَةِ اللهِ وَجَلَالِهِ- سُبْحَانَه وتَعَالَى- مَعَ نَفْيِ مُمَاثَلَتِهَا لِصِفَاتِ الْمَخْلُوقِين. قَالَ تَعَالَى: ﴿وَلِلهِ الْأَسْمَاءُ الْحُسْنَى فَادْعُوهُ بِهَا﴾ [الأعراف: 180]. وَقَالَ تَعَالَى: ﴿قُلِ ادْعُوا اللهَ أَوِ ادْعُوا الرَّحْمَٰنَ ۖ أَيًّا مَّا تَدْعُوا فَلَهُ الْأَسْمَاءُ الْحُسْنَىٰ﴾ [الإسْراء: 110].

وَقَالَ تَعَالَى: ﴿لَيْسَ كَمِثْلِهِ شَيْءٌ وَهُوَ السَّمِيعُ الْبَصِيرُ﴾ [الشّورى: 11].

A Muslim must have confirmed belief in the Beautiful Names and High Attributes of Allah, which were revealed in the Holy Qur'an and the authentic Sunnah of the Prophet Muhammed, peace be upon him. A Muslim takes the Attributes of Allah without any change to their meaning and accepts them in a way that pleases Almighty Allah. None whatsoever is like Him in His Most High Attributes. Allah Almighty said: "And to Allah belong the most Beautiful Names, so call on Him by them." [7: 180]. In another verse, Allah said: "Say (O Muhammad) Call upon Allah or call upon the Most Merciful, by whichever name you call Him, to Him belongs the Most Beautiful Names." [17: 110]. In another verse, Allah said: "There is nothing (whatsoever) like Him, and He is the All-Hearer, the All-Seer." [42: 11].

أسْمَاءُ اللهِ الحُسْنَى
The Most Beautiful Names of Allah

مِنْ عَقِيدَةِ أَهْلِ السُّنَّةِ وَالجَمَاعَةِ الإقْرَارُ وَالإيمَانُ بِكُلِّ مَا وَرَدَ فِي القُرْآنِ الكَرِيمِ وَصَحَّ فِي السُّنَّةِ النّبوِيَّة مِنْ أسْمَاءِ اللهِ الحُسْنَى وَصِفَاتِه العُلَا. قَالَ اللهُ تَعَالَى: ﴿ قُلِ ادْعُوا اللَّهَ أَوِ ادْعُوا الرَّحْمَٰنَ ۖ أَيًّا مَّا تَدْعُوا فَلَهُ الْأَسْمَاءُ الْحُسْنَىٰ ﴾ [الإسراء: 110].

وَقَالَ رَسُولُ اللهِ، صلى الله عليه وسلم: ((إِنَّ لِلهِ تِسْعَةً وَتِسْعِينَ اسْمًا مِائَةً إِلَّا وَاحِدًا مَنْ أَحْصَاهَا دَخَلَ الْجَنَّةَ)) [رَواهُ البُخاري ومُسْلِم].

قَالَ الْعُلَمَاءُ: هَذَا الْحَدِيث، لَا يَدُلُّ عَلَى أَنَّ أسْمَاءَ الله تَعَالَى مَحْصُورَةٌ بِعَدَدٍ مُعَيَّن، وَإِنَّمَا الْمَقْصُودُ أَنَّ هَذِهِ التِّسْعَةَ وَالتِّسْعِينَ مَنْ أَحْصَاهَا دَخَلَ الْجَنَّةَ.

It is the doctrine of the righteous Muslims to recognize and to believe in all the Most Beautiful Names of Allah that are mentioned in the Holy Qur'an and the authentic Sunnah.
Allah said: "Say (O Muhammad) Call upon Allah or call upon the Most Merciful (Allah). Whichever name you call upon, to Him belong the most Beautiful Names." [17: 110].
The Messenger of Allah, peace be upon him, said: "Allah has ninety-nine names, a hundred minus one. Anyone who counted them (memorized them) will enter Paradise." [Al-Bukhari and Muslim].

The scholars said: "This Hadith does not mean the names of Allah are limited to a specific number, rather this Hadith is intended to mean that, whoever memorizes the ninety-nine Name of Allah will enter Paradise."

The Beautiful Names of Allah - أَسْمَاءُ اللهِ الحُسْنَى

القُدُّوسُ	المَلِكُ	الرَّحِيمُ	الرَّحْمَنُ	اللهُ
الجَبَّارُ	العَزِيزُ	المُهَيْمِنُ	المُؤْمِنُ	السَّلَامُ
الغَفَّارُ	المُصَوِّرُ	البَارِئُ	الخَالِقُ	المُتَكَبِّرُ
العَلِيمُ	الفَتَّاحُ	الرَّازِقُ	الوَهَّابُ	القَهَّارُ
المُعِزُّ	الرَّافِعُ	الخَافِضُ	البَاسِطُ	القَابِضُ
العَدْلُ	الحَكَمُ	البَصِيرُ	السَّمِيعُ	المُذِلُّ
الغَفُورُ	العَظِيمُ	الحَلِيمُ	الخَبِيرُ	اللَّطِيفُ
المُقِيتُ	الحَفِيظُ	الكَبِيرُ	العَلِيُّ	الشَّكُورُ
المُجِيبُ	الرَّقِيبُ	الكَرِيمُ	الجَلِيلُ	الحَسِيبُ
البَاعِثُ	المَجِيدُ	الوَدُودُ	الحَكِيمُ	الوَاسِعُ
المَتِينُ	القَوِيُّ	الوَكِيلُ	الحَقُّ	الشَّهِيدُ
المُعِيدُ	المُبْدِئ	المُحْصِي	الحَمِيدُ	الوَلِيُّ
الوَاجِدُ	القَيُّومُ	الحَيُّ	المُمِيتُ	المُحْيِي
المُقْتَدِرُ	القَادِرُ	الصَّمَدُ	الوَاحِدُ	المَاجِدُ
الظَّاهِرُ	الآخِرُ	الأَوَّلُ	المُؤَخِّرُ	المُقَدِّمُ
التَّوَابُ	البَرُّ	المُتَعَالِي	الوَالِي	البَاطِنُ
ذُو الْجَلَالِ وَالْإِكْرَامِ	مَالِكُ المُلْكِ	الرَّؤُوفُ	العَفُوُّ	المُنْتَقِمُ
المَانِعُ	المُغْنِيُّ	الغَنِيُّ	الجَامِعُ	المُقْسِطُ
البَدِيعُ	الهَادِي	النُّورُ	النَّافِعُ	الضَّارُّ
البَاقِي		الرَّشِيدُ	الوَارِثُ	الصَّبُورُ

مَرَاتِبُ الدِّيـنِ
The Levels of Religion

مَرَاتِبُ الدِّيـنِ ثَلَاثَةٌ:
(الْإسْلَامُ وَالْإيمَانُ وَالْإحْسَانُ)

The Levels of Religion are Three:
(Islam, Iman (Faith), and Ihsaan (Excellence)

مَرَاتِبُ الدِّيـنِ ثَلاثَة
The three levels of Religion

1-**Islam** has five pillars 2-**Iman** (Faith) has six pillars 3-**Ihsan** (Excellence) has one pillar	1-الإِسْـلَامُ وَلَهُ خَمْسَةُ أَرْكَانٍ 2-الإِيمَـانُ وَلَهُ سِتَّـةُ أَرْكَانٍ 3-الإحْسَانُ وَلَهُ رُكْنٌ وَاحِـدٌ

Islam الإِسْـلَام

الإسْلَامُ: هُوَ الاسْتِسْلَامُ لِلهِ بِالطَّاعَةِ وَالتَّوْحِيدِ وَالانْقِيَادِ وَالْخُضُوعِ لِأَوَامِرِهِ، وَالابْتِعَادِ عَنِ الشِّرْكِ وَالْأَهْوَاءِ وَالشُّبُهَاتِ.

وَاعْلَمْ أَنَّ الدِّينَ عِنْدَ اللهِ الإِسْلَام، قَالَ اللهُ تَعَالَى: ﴿إِنَّ الدِّينَ عِندَ اللهِ الإِسْلَامُ﴾ [آلِ عِمْرَان: 19]، وَأَخْبَرَ سُبْحَانَهُ وَتَعَالَى أَنَّهُ لَا دِينَ مَقْبُولٌ عِنْدَهُ إِلَّا الإِسْلَام. قَالَ تَعَالَى: ﴿وَمَن يَبْتَغِ غَيْرَ الإِسْلَامِ دِينًا فَلَن يُقْبَلَ مِنْهُ وَهُوَ فِي الآخِرَةِ مِنَ الْخَاسِرِينَ﴾. [آلِ عِمْرَان: 85].

Islam is the surrender to Allah, the Exalted and Almighty, by submission and obedience to His commands. And by worshiping Him alone and to stay away from polytheism, doubt, and self-desire. Also, you should know and be aware that the religion with Allah is Islam, and He does not accept any other religion. Allah Almighty said: "Verily, the religion with Allah is Islam." [3: 19]. In another verse, Allah said: "And whoever seeks a religion other than Islam, it will never be accepted from him; and in the Hereafter, he will be among the losers." [3:85].

أَرْكَانُ الإِسْلَام الخَمْسَة **The Five Pillars of Islam**
1- الشَّهَدَتَان: أَنْ تَشْهَدَ أَنْ لَا إِلَـهَ إِلَّا اللهُ وَأَنَّ مُحَمَّدًا رَسُولُ اللهِ. **1-Ashahadatan** (Declaration of faith): To bear witness that there is no true god but Allah (only Allah has the right to be worshiped) and Muhammad is the Messenger of Allah.
2- الصَّلاة: أَنْ تُقِيمَ الصَّلَوَات المَفْرُوضَة (خَمْسُ صَلَوَاتٍ فِي اليَوْمِ) **2- Salah (The Prayer):** To perform the compulsory prayers (the five daily prayers)
3- الزَّكَاة: أَنْ تُؤتِيَ الزَّكَاة كُلّ سَنَةٍ حَسْب مَا يَنُصّ عَلَيْهِ الشَّرْع **3-Zakah (Obligatory Charity):** To pay the obligatory charity every year according to Islamic rules of Zakah.
4- الصَّوْمُ: أَنْ تَصُومَ شَهْرَ رَمَضَانَ، كُلّ يَوْم مِنْ طُلُوعِ الفَجْرِ الصَّادِقِ إِلَى غُرُوبِ الشَّمْسِ. **4- Sawum (The Fasting):** To fast the month of Ramadan, every day from dawn to sunset.
5- الْحَجُّ: أَنْ تَحُجَّ الْبَيْتَ الحَرَام إِنِ اسْتَطَعْتَ إِلَيْهِ سَبِيلًا، مَرَّةً وَاحِدَةً فِي الْعُمْرِ. **5- Hajj (Pilgrimage):** To perform Pilgrimage to the House of Allah (at Makkah), if you can do so. (Obligatory is one time in your life).

The Iman – الإِيمَـان

الْإيمَانُ: هُوَ الْاعْتِقاد الْجَازِمُ، وَالْإقْرَارُ، وَالتَّصْدِيقُ بِكُلِّ مَا وَرَد فِي الْقُرْآنِ الْكَرِيمِ، وَصَحَّ عَنِ الرَّسُولِ صلى الله عليه وسلم.

فَالْإيمَان اِعْتِقَادٌ بِالْجَنَانِ (الْقَلْب)، وَنُطْقٌ بِاللِّسَانِ، وَعَمَلٌ بِالْجَوَارِحِ، وَالْأرْكَان، يَزِيدُ بِالطَّاعَةِ وَيَنْقُصُ بِالْمَعْصِيَةِ، وَالإيمَانُ لَهُ سِتَّةُ أرْكَانٍ.

Iman (Faith) is the firm belief of all that is in the Holy Qur'an and the authentic Sunnah of the Prophet, peace be upon him. It is a belief in the heart and to utter by tongue the two testimonies and to perform the pillars of Islam. The faith increases by obedience (doing good deeds) and decreases by committing sins, and faith has six pillars, as shown below.

The Six Pillars of Islam	أَرْكَانُ الإيمَان السِّتَة
1. To believe in Allah **2.** and His angels **3.** and His books **4.** and His messengers **5.** and The Last Day **6.** and to believe in the Divine Decree, Qadr, (its good, and its bad).	**1.** أنْ تُؤْمِنَ: بِاللهِ **2.** وَمَلَائِكَتِهِ **3.** وَكُتُبِهِ **4.** وَرُسُلِهِ **5.** وَالْيَوْمِ الْآخِرِ **6.** وَأَنْ تُؤْمِنَ بِالْقَدرِ خَيْرِهِ وَشَرِّهِ

The Iman Branches - شُعَبُ الإيمَـانِ

قَالَ صلى الله عليه وسلم: ((الْإيمَانُ بِضْعٌ وَسَبْعُونَ، أَوْ بِضْعٌ وَسِتُّونَ شُعْبَةً، فَأَفْضَلُهَا قَوْلُ: لَا إِلَـهَ إِلَّا اللهُ، وَأَدْنَاهَا إِمَاطَةُ الأَذَى عَنِ الطَّرِيقِ، وَالْحَيَاءُ شُعْبَةٌ مِنَ الْإيمَانِ)) [الْبُخَارِي وَمُسْلِم].

Branches of Iman: The Prophet, peace be upon him, said: “The Iman (faith) is about seventy or sixty branches, the highest of it is the saying: there is no god but Allah, and the lowest of it is removing anything harmful from the road, and Modesty is a branch of Faith.” [Al-Bukhari and Muslim].

حَلَاوَةُ الإيمَان
The Sweetness of Iman

عَنْ أَنَسِ بْنِ مَالِكٍ رَضِيَ اللهُ عَنْهُ، عَنِ النَّبِيِّ ﷺ قَالَ: ((ثَلَاثٌ مَنْ كُنَّ فِيهِ وَجَدَ حَلَاوَةَ الْإِيمَانِ: أَنْ يَكُونَ اللهُ وَرَسُولُهُ أَحَبَّ إِلَيْهِ مِمَّا سِوَاهُمَا، وَأَنْ يُحِبَّ الْمَرْءَ لاَ يُحِبُّهُ إِلَّا لِلهِ، وَأَنْ يَكْرَهَ أَنْ يَعُودَ فِي الْكُفْرِ كَمَا يَكْرَهُ أَنْ يُقْذَفَ فِي النَّارِ)) [البُخارِي وَمُسْلِم].

The Sweetness of Iman: The Prophet, peace be upon him, said: "There are three qualities whoever attain them will taste the sweetness of Faith (Iman): To love Allah and His Messenger more than anyone else; he loves others only for the sake of Allah; and he hates to return to infidelity after Allah has saved him from it as he would hate to be thrown into the fire (Hell Fire)." [Al-Bukhari and Muslim].

Ihsan (Excellence) - الإحْسَان

الإحْسَانُ هُوَ أَعْلَى مَرَاتِبِ الدِّينِ وَلَهُ رُكْنٌ وَاحِدٌ، وَهُوَ أَنْ تَعْبُدَ اللهَ كَأَنَّكَ تَرَاهُ فَإِنْ لَمْ تَكُنْ تَرَاهُ فَإِنَّهُ يَرَاكَ.

Ihsan (Excellence) is the highest level of religion (to do excellently in the act of worship), and it has one pillar. It is to worship Allah as if you see Him, though you cannot see Him, certainly He sees you.

الفِقْه

The Fiqh

قَالَ النَّبِيُّ صلى الله عليه وسلم :

((مَنْ يُرِدِ اللهُ بِهِ خَيْرًا يُفَقِّهْهُ فِي الدِّين))

"When Allah wishes good for someone, He bestows upon him the understanding of religion."

[Al-Bukhari and Muslim] [البُخارِي وَمُسْلِم]

Purity - الطَّهـارَةُ

حَثَّ الإسْلَامُ عَلَى طَهَارَةِ الْقَلْبِ مِنَ الشِّرْكِ وَالذُّنُوبِ، وَطَهارَةِ الْبَدَنِ وَالثِّيَابِ وَالْمَكَانِ، مِنَ النَّجَاسَةِ وَالأوْسَاخِ. قَالَ اللهُ تَعَالَى: ﴿إِنَّ اللَّهَ يُحِبُّ التَّـوَّابِينَ وَيُحِبُّ الْمُتَطَهِّرِينَ﴾ [البَقَرة: 222].

وَقَالَ النَّبِيُّ صلى الله عليه وسلم: ((الطَّهُورُ شَطْرُ الإِيمَانِ)) [رَواهُ مُسْلِم].

Islam urged Muslims to purify their hearts of polytheism, sins, and to purify their bodies, clothes, and place (of prayer) from impurity and dirt. Allah said: "Allah loves those who repent and loves those who purify themselves." [2: 222].

The Prophet, peace be upon him, said: "Purification is half of the Iman (faith)." [Narrated by Muslim].

الطَّهَارَةُ مِنَ الحَدَثَيْن
Purification from Events

تَجِبُ الطَّهَارَة مِنَ الْحَدَثَيْنِ:

الحَدَثِ الأكْبَرِ (الْجَنَابَةِ وَالْحَيْضِ وَالنِّفَاسِ) وَهَذَا يَسْتَوْجِبُ الْغُسْلَ.

قَالَ تَعَالَى: ﴿وَإِنْ كُنْتُمْ جُنُبًا فَاطَّهَّرُوا﴾ [المَائِدَة: 6].

وَالْحَدَثِ الأصْغَرِ (خُرُوج شَيْء مِنْ أَحَدِ السَّبِيلَيْنِ، وَ زَوَالُ الْعَقْلِ، وأَكْلُ لَحْمِ الإبِلِ)(1)، وَهَذَا يَسْتَوْجِبُ الْوُضُوء، ويَكُون ذَلِكَ بِاسْتِخْدَامِ الْمَاء الْمُطْلَق (مَاء الْمَطَرِ وَالْعُيُون ومَاء الْبَحْر).

قَالَ تَعَالَى: ﴿وَأَنْزَلْنَا مِنَ السَّمَاءِ مَاءً طَهُورًا﴾ [الفُرْقان: 48].

وَقَالَ رَسُولُ اللهِ ﷺ فِي الْبَحْرِ: ((هُوَ الطَّهُورُ مَاؤُهُ، الْحِلُّ مَيْتَتُهُ))

[أَخْرَجَهُ الأَرْبَعَةُ: أبوداود والتِّرمذي والنّسائي، وابن ماجه].

(1) ذهبَ المالِكيّة والحنفِيّة وقول للشّافعي إلى أنّ أكل لحم الإبل لا ينقض الوُضوء.

Purification must be from Events

Major impurity: (Janabah due to the sexual act, menstruation, and puerperium requires ghusl (taking a bath).
Allah said: "If you are in a state of janabah (from sexual act), then Purify yourselves." [5: 6].
Minor impurity: the excretion of anything from the two private parts (urine and feces) or loss of consciousness or eating camel's meat[1] requires Wudu (ablution). In both cases (major or minor impurity), pure water (rainwater, groundwater, and seawater) is to be used for purification. Allah Said: (and We send down pure water from the sky) [25: 48]. And the Prophet, peace be upon him, said about the sea: "Its water is pure, and its dead animals are lawful (to eat)." [Abu Dawud, Tirmidhi, Nasai, and Ibn Majah].

Ablution – الْوُضُوءُ

الْوُضُوءُ عِبَادَةٌ وَهُوَ شَرْطٌ فِي صِحَّةِ الصَّلَاةِ. قَالَ تَعَالَى: ﴿يَا أَيُّهَا الَّذِينَ آمَنُوا إِذَا قُمْتُمْ إِلَى الصَّلَاةِ فَاغْسِلُوا وُجُوهَكُمْ وَأَيْدِيَكُمْ إِلَى الْمَرَافِقِ وَامْسَحُوا بِرُءُوسِكُمْ وَأَرْجُلَكُمْ إِلَى الْكَعْبَيْنِ﴾ [المَائِدَة: 6].

وَجَاءَ فِي صَحِيحِ البُخَارِي بَاب ((لَا تُقْبَلُ صَلَاةٌ بِغَيْرِ طُهُورٍ)).

The Wudu (ablution) is a form of worship and a condition in the validity of prayer. Allah said: "O you who believe! When you stand for the prayer, wash your faces and your hands to the elbows, wipe your heads (with water), and (wash) your legs (feet) to the ankles." [5: 6]. And in Saheeh Al-Bukhari a chapter called: "Prayer is not accepted, without ablution."

(1) Al-Malikiyah, Hanafiyyah, and one saying by Al-Shafi'i said hat eating camel meat does not invalidate ablution.

How to Perform Ablutions	كَيْفِيَّةُ الْوُضُوء
1- Make the intention, then say Bismillah "in the name of Allah."	1- اِنْوِ الْوُضُوءَ، ثُمَّ قُلْ: بِسْمِ اللهِ.
2- Wash the hands up to the wrist.	2- غَسْلُ الْيَدَيْنِ إِلَى الرُّسْغَيْنِ.
3- Rinse the mouth out with water, three times.	3- الْمَضْمَضَة ثَلَاثُ مَرَّاتٍ
4- Sniff the water into your nose and release it out, 3-times.	4- الْإِسْتِنْشَاقُ وَالْإِسْتِنْثَارُ ثَلَاثُ مَرَّاتٍ.
5- Wash the face, three times.	5- غَسْلُ الْوَجْهِ ثَلَاثُ مَرَّاتٍ
6- Wash the hands up to the elbows, three times.	6- غَسْلُ الْيَدَيْنِ إِلَى الْمِرْفَقَيْنِ ثَلَاثُ مَرَّاتٍ.
7- Wet the hands and wipe the head from the front hairline to the back, then return your hands to the front, one time.	7- مَسْحُ الرَّأسِ مَرَّة واحِدَةً، مِنَ الْأَمَامِ إِلَى الْخَلْفِ ثُمَّ يَعُودُ بِيَدَيْهِ إِلَى الأَمَامِ.
8- Wet the hands and wipe the ears inside and outside, once, and it is permissible to renew the water to wipe the ears again.	8- مَسْحُ الْأُذُنَيْنِ مَرَّة وَاحِدَة، وَيُسَنُّ تَجْدِيدُ الْمَاءِ لِمَسْحِ الأُذُنَيْنِ.
9- Wash the feet up to the ankles including washing between the toes, three times.	9- غَسْلُ الرِّجْلَيْنِ (الْقَدَمَيْن) إِلَى الْكَعْبَيْنِ مَعَ تَخْلِيلِ الْمَاءِ بَيْنَ الْأَصَابِعِ، ثَلَاثَ مَرَّاتٍ.

التَّيَمُّم
Tayamum

يَسَّرَ اللهُ تَعَالَى لِعِبَادِهِ مَشْرُوعِيَّةَ التَّيَمُّمِ، وَهُوَ اِسْتِخْدَامُ التُّرَابِ الطَّاهِرِ فِي حَالَةِ عَدَمِ وُجُودِ الْمَاءِ، أَوِ الْعَجْزِ عَنِ اِسْتِعْمَالِهِ بِسَبَبِ الْمَرَضِ أَوْ غَيْرِهِ، وَاعْلَمْ أَنَّ التَّيَمُّمَ يَقُومُ مَقَامَ الْوُضُوءِ وَالْغُسْلِ فِي رَفْعِ الحَدَثِ. قَالَ تَعَالَى: ﴿وَإِنْ كُنْتُمْ مَرْضَىٰ أَوْ عَلَىٰ سَفَرٍ أَوْ جَاءَ أَحَدٌ مِنْكُمْ مِنَ الْغَائِطِ أَوْ لَامَسْتُمُ النِّسَاءَ فَلَمْ تَجِدُوا مَاءً فَتَيَمَّمُوا صَعِيدًا طَيِّبًا فَامْسَحُوا بِوُجُوهِكُمْ وَأَيْدِيكُمْ﴾ [النّساء: 43].

وَقَالَ صلى الله عليه وسلم: ((وَجُعِلَتْ لِي الْأَرْضُ مَسْجِدًا وَطَهُورًا)) [البُخارِي].

Allah made it easy for His servants to use Tayamum. It is the use of pure soil in the absence of water or when water cannot be used because of illness. And know that Tayammum is used instead of wudu and ghusl.

Allah said: “And if you are sick or on a journey or you have come from a place of relieving yourself, or you have contacted women (had a sexual relationship) and find no water (to perform purification), then perform Tayammum, by striking clean earth and wiping your face and your hands (with it).” [4: 43]. The Prophet, peace be upon him, said: “The land has been made for me, as a masjid (mosque) and as purification.” [Al-Bukhari].

How to Perform Tayammum– كَيْفِيَّةُ التَّيَمُّم

أَوَّلًا انْوِ رَفْعَ الْحَدَثِ ثُمَّ اضْرِبِ الْأَرْضَ بِيَدَيْكَ ضَرْبَةً وَاحِدَةً ثُمَّ امْسَحْ بِهِمَا وَجْهَكَ وَكَفَّيْكَ (امْسَحْ كَفَّيْكَ بَعْضَهُمَا بِبَعْضٍ)، فَقَدْ صَحَّ أَنَّ رَسُولَ اللهِ، صلى الله عليه وسلم، قَالَ لِعَمَّارِ بْنِ يَاسِرٍ: ((إِنَّمَا كَانَ يَكْفِيكَ أَنْ تَقُولَ بِيَدَيْكَ هَكَذَا، ثُمَّ ضَرَبَ بِيَدَيْهِ الأَرْضَ ضَرْبَةً وَاحِدَةً، ثُم مَسَحَ الشِّمَالَ عَلَى الْيَمِينِ وَظَاهِرَ كَفَّيْهِ وَوَجْهَهُ)) [البُخارِي وَمُسْلِم].

One should make the intention to purify himself using Tayammum, then strike clean earth with his hands once and then wipe the face and hands (wipe the hands one with the other). It has been reported that the Messenger of Allah, peace be upon him, said to Ammar ibn Yasir: "It would have been sufficient for you to do with it this way, then he, peace be upon him, struck the earth with his hands one time and wiped his face and hands". [Al-Bukhari and Muslim].

بَعْضُ الْعُلَمَاءِ قَالُوا:

1- يُمْكِن اِسْتِخْدَام ضَرْبَتَيْنِ إِحْدَاهُمَا لِلْوَجْهِ وَالْأُخْرَى لِلْكَفَّيْنِ، لَكِنَّ الْأَفْضَلَ ضَرْبَةً وَاحِدَةً كَمَا وَرَدَ فِي الحَدِيث.

2- يُمْكِنُ التَّيَمُّم بِالْحِجَارَةِ وَالأَفْضَل بِالتُّرَابِ إِنْ وُجِدَ.

Some scholars have said:

1- It is permissible to strike the ground twice, one for the face and the other for the hands, but it is better to strike only one, as reported in the Hadith.

2- It is permissible to use rocks for Tayammum, but it is better to use sand if it is available.

Call to Prayer – الأذَانُ	
Allah is the Greatest, Allah is the Greatest. Allah is the Greatest, Allah is the Greatest.	اللهُ أَكْبَـرُ، اللهُ أَكْبَـرُ اللهُ أَكْبَـرُ، اللهُ أَكْبَـرُ
I bear witness that there is no god but Allah I bear witness that there is no god but Allah.	أَشْهَدُ أَنْ لَا إِلَـهَ إِلَّا اللهُ أَشْهَدُ أَنْ لَا إِلَـهَ إِلَّا اللهُ
I bear witness that Muhammad is the messenger of Allah I bear witness that Muhammad is the messenger of Allah	أَشْهَدُ أَنَّ مُحَمَّـدًا رَسُولُ اللهِ أَشْهَدُ أَنَّ مُحَمَّـدًا رَسُولُ اللهِ
Come to the prayer, Come to the prayer.	حَيَّ عَلَى الصَّلَاةِ حَيَّ عَلَى الصَّلَاةِ
Come to success, Come to success.	حَيَّ عَلَى الْفَلَاحِ حَيَّ عَلَى الْفَلَاحِ
Allah is the Greatest, Allah is the Greatest.	اللهُ أَكْبَـرُ، اللهُ أَكْبَـرُ
There is no god but Allah.	لَا إِلَـهَ إِلَّا اللهُ

Important Notes - مُلاحَظَات مُهِمَّة

(1) فِي أَذَانِ صَلَاةِ الْفَجْرِ يَقُولُ الْمُؤَذِّنُ بَعْدَ (حَيَّ عَلَى الْفَلَاحِ، حَيَّ عَلَى الْفَلَاحِ): (الصَّلَاةُ خَيْرٌ مِنَ النَّوْمِ، الصَّلَاةُ خَيْرٌ مِنَ النَّوْمِ)

(1) In the morning Athan (for the Fajr prayer) after saying: "Come to the success, come to the success" then you should say: "Prayer is better than sleep; prayer is better than sleep."

(2) عِنْدَمَا تَسْمَعُ الْأَذَانَ قُلْ: مِثْلَ مَا يَقُولُ الْمُؤَذِّنُ إلاَّ فِي (حَيَّ عَلَى الصَّلاةِ وَحَيَّ عَلَى الفَلَاحِ)، فَقُلْ: (لَا حَوْلَ وَلَا قُوَّةَ إلَّا بِاللهِ).

(2) When you hear the Athan, repeat what the caller says, except when he says (come to the prayer and come to the success) one should say: "La hawla wala quwata illa Bellah.", which means: there is neither power nor might except by Allah.

(3) بَعْدَ الْإِنْتِهَاءِ مِنَ الْأَذَانِ قُلْ: ((اللَّهُمَّ رَبَّ هَذِهِ الدَّعْوَةِ التَّامَّةِ، وَالصَّلَاةِ الْقَائِمَةِ، آتِ مُحَمَّدًا الْوَسِيلَةَ وَالْفَضِيلَةَ، وَابْعَثْهُ مَقَامًا مَحْمُودًا الَّذِي وَعَدْتَهُ)) [البُخارِي].

(3) After the Athan, one should say: "O Allah, the Lord of this perfect call and this established prayer, grant Muhammad the highest place in Paradise, the highest favor, and raise him to the honored place, that You have promised." [Al-Bukhari].

Call to Prayer الإِقَامَةُ	
Allah is the Greatest, Allah is the Greatest.	اللهُ أَكْبَـرُ، اللهُ أَكْبَـرُ
I bear witness that there is no god but Allah.	أَشْهَدُ أَنْ لَا إِلَـهَ إِلَّا اللهُ
I bear witness that Muhammad is the messenger of Allah	أَشْهَدُ أَنَّ مُحَمَّـدًا رَسُولُ اللهِ
Come to the prayer, Come to success.	حَيَّ عَلَى الصَّلَاةِ حَيَّ عَلَى الْفَلَاحِ
Prayer has started, Prayer has started.	قَدْ قَامَتِ الصَّلَاةُ قَدْ قَامَتِ الصَّلَاةُ
Allah is the Greatest, Allah is the Greatest.	اللهُ أَكْبَـرُ، اللهُ أَكْبَـرُ
There is no god but Allah.	لَا إِلَـهَ إِلَّا اللهُ

Attashahud - التَّشَـهُّدُ

التَّشَهُّدُ الأَوَّلُ: بَعْدَ الْقِيَامِ مِنَ السُّجُودِ فِي الرَّكْعَةِ الثَّانِيَةِ، مِنَ الصَّلَاةِ الثُّلَاثِيَّةِ وَالرُّبَاعِيَّةِ قُلْ: ((التَّحِيَّاتُ لِلهِ وَالصَّلَوَاتُ وَالطَّيِّبَاتُ، السَّلَامُ عَلَيْكَ أَيُّهَا النَّبِيُّ وَرَحْمَةُ اللهِ وَبَرَكَاتُهُ، السَّلَامُ عَلَيْنَا وَعَلَى عِبَادِ اللهِ الصَّالِحِينَ، أَشْهَدُ أَنْ لَا إِلَـهَ إِلَّا اللهُ، وَأَشْهَدُ أَنَّ مُحَمَّدًا عَبْدُهُ وَرَسُولُهُ)) (1) [البُخارِي ومُسْلِم].

التَّشَهُّدُ الثَّانِي: فِي نِهَايَةِ الصَّلَاةِ وَقَبْلَ التَّسْلِيمِ اِقْرَأْ التَّشَهُّدَ الأَوَّلَ ثُمَّ أَضِفْ إِلَيْهِ: ((اللَّهُمَّ صَلِّ عَلَى مُحَمَّدٍ وَعَلَى آلِ مُحَمَّدٍ، كَمَا صَلَّيْتَ عَلَى إِبْرَاهِيمَ وَعَلَى آلِ إِبْرَاهِيمَ، إِنَّكَ حَمِيدٌ مَجِيدٌ، اللَّهُمَّ بَارِكْ عَلَى مُحَمَّدٍ وَعَلَى آلِ مُحَمَّدٍ، كَمَا بَارَكْتَ عَلَى إِبْرَاهِيمَ وَعَلَى آلِ إِبْرَاهِيمَ، إِنَّكَ حَمِيدٌ مَجِيدٌ)) [البُخارِي ومُسْلِم].

First Tashahud: After the second Rakah recite while seating: "All Greetings, Prayers, and Pure actions are belonging to Allah. The Blessings and the mercy of Allah are on the Prophet; peace be on us, and the good slaves of Allah. I testify that there is no god but Allah and I testify that Muhammad is the slave and messenger of Allah." [Al-Bukhari and Muslim].

Second Tashahud: At the end of the prayer and before Tassleem, recite the first Tashahud, and then say: "O Allah! Bless Muhammad and the family of Muhammad; as you have blessed Abraham and the family of Abraham. Surely You are the Praised and Glorified. O Allah! Be gracious unto Muhammad and the family of Muhammad as you were gracious unto Abraham and the family of Abraham. Surely You are the Most Praised, the Most Glorious." [Al-Bukhari and Muslim].

There are other authentic forms of Tashahud - (1) هُناك صِيَغ أُخْرى صَحِيحة لِلتَّشَهّد

Prayer الصَّلَاةُ

الصَّلَاةُ هِيَ أُمُّ الْعِبَادَاتِ وَأعْظَمُ أَرْكَانِ الْإسْلَامِ بَعْدَ الشَّهَادَتَيْنِ، وَلَهَا مَنْزِلَةٌ كَبِيرَةٌ عِنْدَ اللهِ، عَزَّ وَجَلَّ. فَالصَّلَاةُ صِلَةٌ بَيْنَ الْعَبدِ وَرَبِّهِ، وَهِيَ عَمُودُ الدِّينِ، وَلَا حَظَّ فِي الْإسْلَامِ لِمَن تَرَكَهَا.

فَرَضَ اللهُ - سُبْحَانَهُ وَتَعَالَى- الصَّلَاةَ عَلَى كُلِّ مُسْلِمٍ بَالِغٍ عَاقِلٍ، ذَكَرًا أَوْ أُنْثَى، خَمْسَ مَرَّاتٍ فِي الْيَوْمِ وَاللَّيْلَةِ، وَأمَرَ بِالْمُحَافَظَةِ عَلَيْها فِي كُلِّ الْأحْوَالِ وَالْأوْقَاتِ. قَالَ تَعَالَى: ﴿وَأَقِيمُواْ الصَّلَاةَ وَآتُواْ الزَّكَاةَ وَارْكَعُواْ مَعَ الرَّاكِعِينَ﴾ [البَقَرة: 43]. وَعِنْدَمَا سُئِلَ الرَّسُولُ ﷺ، عَنْ أفْضَلِ الْأعْمَال قَالَ: ((الصَّلَاةُ عَلَى وَقْتِهَا)). وَقَدْ تَوَعَّدَ اللهُ بِالْوَيْلِ لِمَنْ يَتَهَاوَنْ وَيَتَسَاهَلْ فِي أمْرِ الصَّلَاةِ، قَالَ تَعَالَى: ﴿فَوَيْلٌ لِلْمُصَلِّينَ * الَّذِينَ هُمْ عَنْ صَلَاتِهِمْ سَاهُونَ﴾ [الماعُون: 4-5]

Prayer is the mother of worship and the greatest pillars of Islam after the two testimonies (declaration of faith). Prayer is a link between the servant and his Lord. It has a great status with Allah Almighty and it is the backbone of Islam and there is no share in Islam for one who abandons it. Allah made the five daily prayers obligatory on every Muslim, adult, and mature and ordered the performance of it in all situations and times. Allah said: “And establish prayer and give Zakah and bow down with those who bow.” [2: 43]. The Prophet, peace be upon him, was asked about the best good deeds, he said: “Performing the prayer on time”. Beware that Allah warned those who are lazy about their prayer by saying:

“So woe to the worshippers, who ignore (or delay), their prayers.” [107: 4-5]

Obligatory Prayers – الصَّلَوَاتُ المَفْرُوضَة	
1- Salatul-Fajr (dawn): **Two Rakah[1]:** Reading loud	**1- صَلَاةُ الْفَجْرِ:** رَكْعَتَانِ جَهْرًا.
2- Salatul-Thuhr (afternoon) **Four Rakah:** Reading silently	**2- صَلَاةُ الظُّهْرِ:** أَرْبَعُ رَكَعَاتٍ سِرًا.
3- Salatul-Asr (late afternoon) **Four Rakah:** Reading silently	**3- صَلَاةُ الْعَصْرِ:** أَرْبَعُ رَكَعَاتٍ سِرًا.
4- Salatul-Maghrib (after sunset). **Three Rakah:** The first two Rakah, reading aloud. The third Rakah, reading silently	**4- صَلَاةُ الْمَغْرِبِ:** ثَلَاثُ رَكَعَاتٍ: الْأُولَى و الثَّانِيَةُ جَهْرًا وَالثَّالِثَةُ سِرًا.
5- Salatul-Isha (night) **Four Rakah:** The first two Rakah, reading aloud. The last two Rakah, reading silently	**5- صَلَاةُ الْعِشَاءِ:** أَرْبَعُ رَكَعَاتٍ: الْأُولَى وَالثَّانِيَةُ جَهْرًا، الثَّالِثَةُ وَالرَّابِعَةُ سِرًا.

(1) Rakah is a unit of prayer, consisting of a bow, standing, and two prostrations.

How to Pray - كَيْفِيَّةُ الصَّلَاة

الصَّلَاةُ عِبَادَةٌ ذَاتِ أَقْوَالٍ وَأَفْعَالٍ، تَبْدَأُ بِالتَّكْبِيرِ وَتَنْتَهِي بِالتَّسْلِيمِ.
يَجِبُ أَنْ تُؤَدَّى الصَّلَاة بِالْكَيْفِيَّةِ الثَّابِتَةِ عَنْ رَسُولِ اللهِ ﷺ، قَالَ ﷺ:
((صَلّوا كَمَا رَأَيْتُمُونِي أُصَلِّي)) [البُخَارِي].

وَالْحَدِيثُ التَّالِي يُبَيِّنُ كَيْفِيَّةَ الصَّلَاة:

قَالَ النَّبِيُّ ﷺ: ((إِذَا قُمْتَ إِلَى الصَّلَاةِ فَأَسْبِغِ الْوُضُوءَ، ثُمَّ اسْتَقْبِلِ الْقِبْلَةَ، فَكَبِّرْ، ثُمَّ اقْرَأْ مَا تَيَسَّرَ مَعَكَ مِنَ الْقُرْآنِ، ثُمَّ ارْكَعْ حَتَّى تَطْمَئِنَّ رَاكِعًا، ثُمَّ ارْفَعْ حَتَّى تَعْتَدِلَ قَائِمًا، ثُمَّ اسْجُدْ حَتَّى تَطْمَئِنَّ سَاجِدًا، ثُمَّ ارْفَعْ حَتَّى تَطْمَئِنَّ جَالِسًا، ثُمَّ اسْجُدْ حَتَّى تَطْمَئِنَّ سَاجِدًا، ثُمَّ افْعَلْ ذَلِكَ فِي صَلَاتِكَ كُلِّهَا)) [البُخَارِي ومُسْلِم].

Prayer is a worship with words and actions. It starts with Takbeer and ends with Tasleem, and performed according to the Sunnah. The Prophet, peace be upon him, said: "Pray as you have seen me praying." [Al-Bukhari].

The following Hadith shows how to pray:

The Prophet, peace be upon him, said: "When you stand for Assalah (prayer), perform Wudu (ablution) thoroughly. Face the Kiblah (Makkah) and make Takbeer (say Allahu-Akbar), then recite what you memorize (from the Qur'an), then bow down until you feel comfortable, then rise from bowing till you stand straight, then prostrate (calmly) until you feel comfortable, then raise (your head) and sit with calmness and then prostrate (calmly) until you feel comfortable. Do the same in all your prayer." [Al-Bukhari and Muslim]

شُرُوطُ الصَّلَاةِ تِسْعَةٌ وَهِيَ:
الإِسْلَامُ، وَالْعَقلُ، وَالتَّمْيِيزُ، وَرَفْعُ الحَدَثِ، وَإِزَالَةُ النَّجَاسَةِ، وَسَتْرُ الْعَوْرَةِ، وَدُخُولُ الْوَقْتِ، وَاسْتِقْبَالُ الْقِبْلَةِ، وَالنِّيَّةُ.

The nine conditions of Salah are:
Islam, sanity, puberty, state of purity, removal of filth (from body, clothes, and place of worship), covering the awrah[1], the entrance of proper time, facing the direction of Qiblah, and intention for the prayer.

(1) **Awrah** is to cover the intimate parts of the body with clothing in the prayer (man's awra is different than woman's awra)

صَلَاتُ الجَمَاعَةِ
Prayer in congregation

عَلَى المُسْلِمِ أَنْ يُحَافِظَ عَلَى الصَّلَاةِ فِي كُلِّ الأَحْوَالِ وَالأَوْقَاتِ وَأَنْ يُصَلِّيَ فِي الْمَسْجِدِ مَا اسْتَطَاعَ لِذَلِكَ سَبِيلًا، فَقَدْ صَحَّ عَنْ رَسُولِ اللهِ ﷺ، أَنَّهُ قَالَ: ((صَلَاةُ الْجَمَاعَةِ أَفْضَلُ مِنْ صَلَاةِ الْفَذِّ بِسَبْعٍ وَعِشْرِينَ دَرَجَةً)) [البُخارِي و مُسْلِم].
أَمَّا المَرْأَةُ المُسْلِمَةُ فَصَلَاتُهَا فِي بَيْتِهَا أَفْضَل، قَالَ ﷺ: ((لاَ تَمْنَعُوا نِسَاءَكُمُ الْمَسَاجِدَ وَبُيُوتُهُنَّ خَيْرٌ لَهُنَّ)) [رَوَاهُ أَبُو دَاود].

A Muslim should guard his obligatory prayers at all times and in all circumstances. A Muslim male also should do his obligatory prayers in the masjid, as long as he is able. The Messenger of Allah, peace be upon him, said: "Prayer in congregation is better than praying alone by twenty-seven degrees." [Al-Bukhari and Muslim].

Muslim women are better for them to pray in their homes. The Prophet, peace be upon him, said: "Do not prevent your women from visiting the mosque; but their houses are better for them (for praying)." [Abu Dawood].

سُنَنُ الصَّلَاةِ الرَّاتِبَة وَفَضْلها
The Confirmed Recommended Voluntary Prayers

وَاظَبَ الرَّسُولُ ﷺ، عَلَى ثِنْتَيْ عَشْرَةَ رَكْعَةً مَعَ الصَّلَوَاتِ الْخَمْس وَبَيَّنَ فَضْلَهَا وَهِيَ:

سُنَنٌ قَبْلِيَّةٌ: وَهِيَ رَكْعَتَانِ قَبْلَ الْفَجْرِ، وَأَرْبَعًا قَبْلَ الظُّهْرِ.

سُنَنٌ بَعْدِيَّةٌ: وَهِيَ رَكْعَتَانِ بَعْدَ الظُّهْرِ، وَرَكْعَتَانِ بَعْدَ الْمَغْرِبِ، وَرَكْعَتَانِ بَعْدَ الْعِشَاءِ.

قَالَ ﷺ: ((مَنْ صَلَّى فِي يَوْمٍ وَلَيْلَةٍ ثِنْتَيْ عَشْرَةَ رَكْعَةً بُنِيَ لَهُ بَيْتٌ فِي الْجَنَّةِ، أَرْبَعًا قَبْلَ الظُّهْرِ، وَرَكْعَتَيْنِ بَعْدَهَا، وَرَكْعَتَيْنِ بَعْدَ الْمَغْرِبِ، وَرَكْعَتَيْنِ بَعْدَ الْعِشَاءِ، وَرَكْعَتَيْنِ قَبْلَ صَلاةِ الْفَجْرِ)) [التِّرمذي وَصَحَّحَه الألباني].

The Prophet, peace be upon him, never left twelve Rak'ahs associated with the five daily prayers. The following Hadith describe them: The Prophet, peace be upon him, said: "Whoever prays additional twelve Rak'ahs during the night and day, a house will be built for him in Paradise: four before Thuhr (afternoon) and two after it, two Rak'ahs after Maghrib (after sunset), two Rak'ahs after 'Isha' (night prayer) and two Rak'ahs before Fajr (dawn prayer)." [al-Tirmidhi].

<u>صَلَاةُ الْوِتْر</u> :أَوْصَى الرَّسُولُ ﷺ، بِالْمُحَافَظَةِ عَلَى صَلَاةِ الْوِتْرِ قَبْلَ النَّوْمِ.

The Prophet, Peace be upon him, strongly recommended doing Witter prayer before sleeping.

أَوْقاتُ النَّهْيِ عَنِ الصَّلَاةِ
Times when it is Forbidden to Pray

نَهَى رَسُولُ اللهِ صلى الله عليه وسلم، عَنِ الصَّلَاةِ فِي الأَوْقَاتِ التَّالِيَةِ:
1- بَعْدَ صَلَاةِ الْفَجْرِ إِلَى طُلُوعِ الشَّمْسِ.
2- عِنْدَمَا تَكُونُ الشَّمْسُ فِي وَسَطِ السَّمَاءِ حَتَّى تَمِيلَ إِلَى الْغَربِ.
3- بَعْدَ صَلَاةِ الْعَصْرِ إِلَى أَنْ تَغِيبَ الشَّمْسُ.
وَالنَّهْيُ عَنِ الصَّلَاةِ يَكُونُ أَشَدّ عِنْدَ الشُّرُوقِ وَالْغُرُوبِ. عَنْ عُقْبَةَ بْنِ عَامِرٍ، رَضِيَ اللهُ عَنْهُ، قَالَ: ((ثَلَاثُ سَاعَاتٍ كَانَ رَسُولُ اللهِ صلى الله عليه وسلم، يَنْهَانَا أَنْ نُصَلِّيَ فِيهِنَّ، أَوْ أَنْ نَقْبُرَ فِيهِنَّ مَوْتَانَا، حِينَ تَطْلُعُ الشَّمْسُ بَازِغَةً حَتَّى تَرْتَفِعَ، وَحِينَ يَقُومُ قَائِمُ الظَّهِيرَةِ حَتَّى تَمِيلَ الشَّمْسُ، وَحِينَ تَضَيَّفُ الشَّمْسُ لِلْغُرُوبِ حَتَّى تَغْرُبَ)) [رَوَاهُ مُسْلِم].

مُلَاحَظَة: يُسْتَثْنَى مِنَ النَّهْيِ:
قَضَاءُ الفَوَائِتِ وَمَا كَانَ لِسَبَبٍ مِثْل: تَحِيَّةُ المَسْجِدِ وَسُنَّةُ الوُضُوءِ.

Three times when it is forbidden to do voluntary prayers:

1- After the dawn prayer until the sun rises.
2- When the sun is in the middle of the sky, until it tends west.
3- After the Asr prayer until the sunset.

The prohibition of prayer is most severe at sunrise and sunset. Ogbah, may Allah be pleased with him, said: “Allah's Messenger, peace be upon him, forbade us to pray or to bury our dead: when the sun has clearly started to rise until it is fully rising, when it is directly overhead at midday until it has passed its zenith, and when the sun starts to set until it has fully set.” [Muslim].

Note: It is permitted to make up the missed prayers and any prayer with a Cause, such as praying two Rak’ahs when you enter the Masjid

Friday Prayer – صَلاةُ الْجُمُعَةِ

يَوْمُ الْجُمُعَةِ خَيْرُ يَوْمٍ طَلَعَتْ عَلَيْهِ الشَّمْسُ، وَهُوَ أَفْضَلُ الأيَامِ عِنْدَ اللهِ تَعَالَى وَفِيهِ سَاعَةٌ لَا يُوَافِقُهَا عَبْدٌ مُسْلِمٌ، وَهُوَ قَائِمٌ يُصَلِّي يَسْأَلُ اللهَ شَيْئًا، إلَّا أعْطَاهُ إيَّاه، وَفِيهِ تُكَفَّرُ الذُّنُوبُ وَالْمَعَاصِي.

أَجْمَعَ الْفُقَهَاءُ عَلَى أنَّ صَلاةَ الْجُمُعَةِ فَرْضُ عَيْنٍ عَلَى الرِّجَالِ بِالْمَسْجِدِ. وَلِهَذا يَنْبَغِي لِلْمُسْلِمِ أنْ يَسْعَى وَيُبَادِرَ لِحُضُورِ صَلَاةِ الْجُمُعَةِ، وَيَتْرُكَ التِّجَارَةِ وَكُلَّ الأعْمَالِ إمْتِثَالًا لِقَوْلِهِ تَعَالَى: ﴿يَا أَيُّهَا الَّذِينَ آمَنُوا إِذَا نُودِيَ لِلصَّلَاةِ مِن يَوْمِ الْجُمُعَةِ فَاسْعَوْا إِلَىٰ ذِكْرِ اللَّهِ وَذَرُوا الْبَيْعَ ۚ ذَٰلِكُمْ خَيْرٌ لَّكُمْ إِن كُنتُمْ تَعْلَمُونَ﴾ [الجُمُعة: 9].

Friday is the best day on which the sun rises, and it is the best day in the sight of Allah. On Friday there is an hour that Allah will accept the supplication from whoever invokes Him. On Friday, Allah gives a great reward for good deeds and wipes sins. The scholars unanimously agreed that Friday prayer is obligatory for men and performed in the Masjid. So, it is recommended to hasten to attend the Friday prayer and to leave the trade and all other acts. Allah said: “O you who believe! When the call for prayer on Friday is made, then hasten to the remembrance of Allah and leave off trading that is best for you, if you do know.” [62: 9].

Warning - تَحْذِير

حَذَّرَ الرَّسُولُ، صلى الله عليه وسلم، مِنَ التَّخَلُّفِ عَنْ صَلَاةِ الْجُمُعَةِ بِقَوْلِهِ:

((لَيَنْتَهِيَنَّ أقْوَامٌ عَنْ وَدْعِهِمُ الْجُمُعَاتِ أَوْ لَيَخْتِمَنَّ اللهُ عَلَى قُلُوبِهِمْ ثُمَّ لَيَكُونَنَّ مِنَ الْغَافِلِينَ)) [رواه مُسْلِم].

Warning:

The Prophet, peace be upon him, warned people who are neglecting Friday prayer. He said: "People need to stop neglecting the Friday prayers or Allah will seal over their hearts and then they will be among the negligent." [Muslim].

كَيْفِيَّةُ صَلاَةِ الْجُمُعَةِ
How to perform Friday Prayer

صَلاَةُ الْجُمُعَةِ لَهَا رُكْنَانِ أَسَاسِيَّانِ هُمَا:

1- خُطْبَتَانِ قَبْلَ الصَّلَاةِ، يَفْصِلُ الإِمَامُ بَيْنَهُمَا بِجِلْسَةٍ قَصِيرَةٍ.

2- الصَّلَاةُ: وَهِيَ رَكْعَتَانِ، يَجْهَرُ الإِمَامُ فِيهِمَا بِالقِرَاءَةِ.

Friday prayer has two main pillars:

1- Two Khutbah before prayer.

2- The prayer is two Rak'ahs (reading loud for the Imam)

Virtues Friday فَضَائِلُ يَوْمِ الْجُمُعَةِ

يَوْمُ الْجُمُعَةِ لَهُ فَضَائِلُ كَثِيرَةٌ، وَهَذِهِ بَعْضُ الْخَصَائِصِ وَالْفَضَائِلِ:

1- الإِكْثَارُ مِنَ الصَّلاة عَلَى النَّبِيِّ، ﷺ.

2- يُسْتَحَبُّ الاغْتِسَالُ، وَالتَّطَيُّبُ، وَلُبْسُ أَحْسَنَ الثِّيَابِ.

3- التَّبْكِيرُ وَالسَّعْيُ لِلصَّلَاة وَتَرْكُ التِّجَارَةِ وَالْبَيْعِ.

4- الحَذَرُ مِنْ تَخَطِّي الرِّقَابِ وَإِيذَاءِ الْمُصَلِّين.

5- يَجِبُ الإِنْصَاتُ لِلْخُطْبَةِ وَيَحْرُمُ الْكَلَامُ أَثْنَاءَهَا.

6- يُسْتَحَبُّ قِرَاءَةُ سُورَةِ الْكَهْفِ يَوْمَ الْجُمُعَةِ أَوْ لَيْلَتِهَا.

7- الدُّعَاءُ: قَالَ ﷺ: ((إِنَّ فِي الْجُمُعَةِ سَاعَةً لا يُوَافِقُهَا عَبْدٌ مُسْلِمٌ يَسْأَلُ اللَّهَ فِيهَا خَيْرًا إِلَّا أَعْطَاهُ إِيَّاهُ)) [البُخارِي و مُسْلِم].

Virtues of Friday

Friday is the best day of all days and has many virtues and etiquettes that Muslims should consider maintaining and practicing them. The following are some Virtues:

1- Invoke prayers for the Prophet; peace be upon him.

2- One should take a shower, and wear the best clothes.

3- It is recommended to go early to the Friday prayer and leave the trading and selling during prayer time.

4- Be careful not to step over people and not to harm them.

5- It is necessary to listen to the Khutbah and to refrain from talking when the Imam is delivering the Khutbah.

6- It is recommended to recite Surat Al- Kahf on Friday.

7- It is recommended to make supplication. The Prophet, peace be upon him, said: "There is an hour on Friday, and if a Muslim gets it while praying and asks Allah something, indeed Allah will grant his supplication." [Al-Bukhari and Muslim].

Eid Prayer - صَلَاةُ العِيد

شَرَعَ اللهُ - سُبْحَانَهُ وَتَعَالَى- لِلْمُسْلِمِين عِيدَيْنِ هُمَا:

1- **عِيدُ الْفِطْرِ** بَعْدَ شَهْرِ رَمَضَانَ - اليَوْمُ الأَوَّلُ مِنْ شَوَّال.

2- **عِيدُ الأَضْحَى** بَعْدَ يَوْمِ عَرَفَة - اليَوْمُ الْعَاشِرُ مِنْ ذِي الحِجَّة.

صَلَاةُ الْعِيدِ سُنَّةٌ مُؤَكَّدَة، يَنْبَغِي الْمُحَافَظَةُ عَلَيْهَا، فَقَدْ وَاظَبَ عَلَيْهَا النَّبِيُّ صلى الله عليه وسلم، وَصَحَّ عَنْهُ أَنَّهُ أَمَرَ الرِّجَالَ وَالنِّسَاءَ أَنْ يَخْرُجُوا لَهَا. وَالأَفْضَلُ أَدَاءهَا فِي المُصَلَّى (خَارِجَ المَسْجِدِ) إنْ كَانَ ذَلِكَ مُمْكِنًا.

Eid Prayer

Allah, the Almighty, has prescribed for Muslims two Eids:

1- Eidul-Fitr, after Ramadan – the first day of Shawwal.

2- Eidul-Adha, after the day of Arafah – the tenth day of Dhul-Hijjah. Allah said: “So perform your prayer to your Lord and sacrifice (to Him alone).” [108: 2].

The Prophet, peace be upon him, has led the Eid prayer continually, and he ordered men and women to observe Eid prayer. It is better to perform the Eid prayer outside the Masjid (in an open space) if that is possible.

كَيْفِيَّةُ صَلَاةِ الْعِيدِ

How to perform Eid Prayer

صَلَاةُ الْعِيدِ رَكْعَتَانِ بِلَا أَذَانٍ وَلَا إِقَامَةٍ، يَجْهَرُ الْإِمَامُ فِيهِمَا بِالْقِرَاءَةِ، وَيُكَبِّرُ سَبْعَ تَكْبِيرَاتٍ فِي الرَّكْعَةِ الأَوْلَى، وَخَمْسَ تَكْبِيرَاتٍ فِي الرَّكْعَةِ الثَّانِيةِ، قَبْلَ قِرَاءَةِ الْفَاتِحَة، وَبَعْدَ الْإِنْتِهَاءِ مِنَ الصَّلَاةِ يَقُومُ الْإِمَامُ وَيَخْطُبُ خُطْبَتَيْنِ، يَفْصِلُ بَيْنَهُمَا بِجَلْسَةٍ قَصِيرَةٍ.

The Eid prayer is two Rak’ahs (with no Athan or Iqamah), and two Kutbah after the prayer and performed as follows:

1- In the first Rak’ah the Imam makes seven times Takbeer “saying Allahu-Akbar” before reading Al-Fateha.

2- In the second Rak’ah the imam makes five times Takbeert before reading Al-Fateha.

3- After the prayer, the Imam stands up and delivers two Khutbah.

Virtues of Eid - آدَابُ صَلَاةِ الْعِيـدِ

1. يُسْتَحَبُّ التَّكْبِيرُ قَبْلَ الصَّلَاةِ: أَحَد صِيَغ التَّكْبِيرِ أَنْ تَقُولَ: (اللهُ أَكْبَرُ اللهُ أَكْبَرُ، لَا إِلَـهَ إلَّا اللهُ، وَاللهُ أَكْبَرُ اللهُ أَكْبَرُ، وَلِلَّهِ الْحَمْدُ).
2. الْغُسْلُ وَالتَّطَيُّبُ وَلبْسُ أَحْسَنَ وَأَجْمَلَ الثِّيَابِ.
3. الْأَكْلُ قَبْلَ الْخُرُوجِ فِي الْفِطْرِ، وَبَعْدَ الصَّلَاةِ فِي الْأَضْحَى.
4. إِخْرَاجُ زَكَاةِ الْفِطْرِ، قَبْلَ صَلَاةِ عِيدِ الْفِطْرِ.
5. خُرُوجُ النِّسَاءِ وَالصِّبْيَانِ لَهَا.
6. الْأَفْضَلُ أَنْ تُقَامَ صَلَاةُ الْعِيدِ فِي الْعَرَاءِ، وَلَا حَرَجَ فِي فِعْلِهَا فِي الْمَسَاجِدِ.
7. يُشْرَعُ قَضَاءُ صَلَاةِ الْعِيـدِ لِمَنْ فَاتَتْهُ.
8- يُهَنِّئُ الْمُسْلِمُ أَخَاهُ الْمُسْلِمَ بِقَوْلِهِ " تَقَبَّـلَ اللهُ مِنَّا وَمِنْكَ".

1. It is recommended to do Takbeer on the day of Eid, by saying: “Allah is the Greatest, Allah is the Greatest, and there is no god but Allah. Allah is the Greatest, Allah is the Greatest, and all praises are for Allah.”.

2. It is recommended to take a shower, groom, and to wear the best clothes.

3. Eating before going out to pray on Eid al-Fitr and after the prayer on Eid al-Adha.

4. Paying Zakatul-Fitr before Eid al-Fitr prayer.

5. Women and children are recommended to attend it.

6. The Eid prayer should be held at an open area if that is possible, if not, then it can be done in the masjid.

7. It is permissible to do Eid prayer if you missed it.

8. Muslim congratulates his brother Muslim by saying: "May Allah accept from us and from you."

Zakah – الزَّكَـاةُ

الزَّكَاةُ أَحَدُ أَرْكَانِ الْإِسْلَامِ الْخَمْسَةِ، وَهِيَ عِبَادَةٌ عَظِيمَةٌ، أَوْجَبَهَا اللهُ عَلَى كُلِّ مُسْلِمٍ حُـرٍّ مَالِكٍ لِلنِّصَاب وَحَالَ عَلَيْهِ الْحَوْلُ الْهِجْرِيُّ.

قَالَ اللهُ تَعَالَى: ﴿وَأَقِيمُوا الصَّلَاةَ وَآتُوا الزَّكَاةَ وَأَطِيعُوا الرَّسُولَ لَعَلَّكُمْ تُرْحَمُونَ﴾ [النُّور:56].

وَقَالَ تَعَالَى: ﴿خُذْ مِنْ أَمْوَالِهِمْ صَدَقَةً تُطَهِّرُهُمْ وَتُزَكِّيهِم بِهَا﴾ [التَّوْبَة: 103].

وَقَالَ صلى الله عليه وسلم: ((بُنِيَ الْإِسْلَامُ عَلَى خَمْسٍ: شَهَادَةِ أَنْ لَا إِلَـهَ إِلَّا اللهُ، وَأَنَّ مُحَمَّـدًا، رَسُولُ اللهِ، وَإِقَامِ الصَّلَاةِ، وَإِيتَاءِ الزَّكَاةِ، وَحَجِّ الْبَيْتِ، وَصَوْمِ رَمَضَانَ)) [رَواهُ البُخارِي ومُسْلِم].

Zakah is one of the five pillars of Islam, and it is a great worship that Allah has enjoined on every free Muslim who owns the nisaab (a certain amount of wealth) and a whole year (Lunar year) has passed on that wealth.
Allah said: “Establish prayer and pay Zakah and obey the Messenger (Muhammad) so that you may receive mercy (from Allah).” [24: 56].
In another verse, Allah said: “Take from their wealth a charity that purifies and sanctifies them with it.” [9: 103]. The Prophet, peace be upon him, said: “Islam built on five pillars: testifying that there is no god but Allah, Muhammad is the Messenger of Allah, performing the prayer, paying Zakah, Performing Pilgrimage to the House of Allah, and fasting the month of Ramadan” [Al-Bukhari and Muslim].

الْأَمْوَالُ الَّتِي تَجِبُ فِيهَا الزَّكَاة
The wealth in which Zakah is due

الزَّكَاةُ فِي الإِسْلَامِ وَاجِبَةٌ فِي:

1- الذَّهَبِ وَالْفِضَّةِ وَالْأَوْرَاقِ النَّقْدِيَّةِ.

2- عُرُوضِ التِّجَارَةِ.

3- الْخَارِجِ مِنَ الْأَرْضِ: الْحُبُوبُ وَالثِّمَارُ وَالْمَعَادِنِ وَالرِّكَازِ.

4- بَهِيمَةِ الْأَنْعَامِ: الإِبِلُ وَالْبَقَرُ وَالْغَنَمُ.

Zakah in Islam is obligatory on the following types:

1- Gold, silver, and currency.

2- Trade goods.

3- Out of the ground: grain, seeds, minerals, and ore.

4- Animals: camels, cattle's and sheep.

Nesab (Quorum) of Zakah - نِصَابُ الزَّكَاةِ

نِصَابُ الزَّكَاةِ هُوَ مِقْدَارٌ مِنَ الْمَالِ حَدَّدَهُ الشَّرْعُ، لَا تَجِبُ الزَّكَاة فِي أَقَلّ مِنْهُ، وتَخْتَلِفُ قِيمَتُهُ حَسْبَ جِنْسِ الْمَالِ. وَقَدْ قُدِّرَ نِصَابُ الذَّهَبِ بِخَمْسَةٍ وَثَمَانِينَ جرَامًا (85 جرَام) مِنَ الذَّهَبِ، وَمِنَ الْفِضَّةِ بِخَمْسِمَائةٍ وَخَمْسَةٍ وَتِسْعِينَ جَرَامًا (595 جَرَام) مِنَ الْفِضّةِ.

إِذَا إِمْتَلَكَ المُسْلِمُ النِّصَابَ (أَوْ أَكْثَرَ) مِنَ الْمَالِ وَحَالَ عَلَيْهِ الْحَوْلُ الْهِجْرِيُّ فَيَجِبُ عَلَيْهِ إِخْرَاجُ الزَّكَاةِ.

مِقْدَارُ زَّكَاة الْمَال رُبْـعُ الْعُشْـرِ (2.5 %) مِنْ كَامِلِ الْمَبْلَغ.

The Nisab (quorum) for Zakah is the minimum amount of wealth specified by Shari'a (Islamic Law) below its value Zakah is not obligatory, and it depends on the type of wealth.

The gold Nisab is eighty-five grams (85 grams) of gold, and for silver is five hundred and ninety-five grams (595 grams) of silver. If the Muslim has a Nisab (or more) of the money and he has it for one complete year, then he must pay the Zakah. The amount of Zakah is two-and-half percent (2.5%) of the full amount of the money.

Note - مُلاحَظَة

لا زَكَاةَ عَنِ الْحَاجَاتِ الضَّرُورِيَّةِ لِلْإِنْسَانِ، كَالمَطْعَمِ، وَالْمَلْبَسِ، وَالْمَسْكَنِ، وَالْمَرْكَبِ.

There is no Zakah on the necessities of man, such as food, drink, clothing, housing, and transportation.

Zakah distributed - مصارِفُ الزَّكَاة

تُصْرَفُ الزَّكَاةُ لِثَمَانِيَّةِ أصْنَافٍ بَيَّنَهَا اللهُ فِي الْقُرْآنِ الْكَرِيمِ: قَالَ تَعَالَى: ﴿إِنَّمَا الصَّدَقَاتُ لِلْفُقَرَاءِ وَالْمَسَاكِينِ وَالْعَامِلِينَ عَلَيْهَا وَالْمُؤَلَّفَةِ قُلُوبُهُمْ وَفِي الرِّقَابِ وَالْغَارِمِينَ وَفِي سَبِيلِ اللهِ وَابْنِ السَّبِيلِ ۖ فَرِيضَةً مِّنَ اللهِ ۗ وَاللهُ عَلِيمٌ حَكِيمٌ﴾ [التَّوْبَة: 60].

Zakah distributed among eight categories, according to the Qur'an. Allah said: "The Zakah is only for the poor and the needy, and those who collect the Zakah and for those newly converted to Islam (whose hearts require attention) and to free the captives; And for those in debt; And for Allah's Cause; And for the wayfarer; It is an ordinance from Allah; and Allah is All-Knowing, All-Wise." [9: 60].

Zakatul-Fitr - زَكَاةُ الفِطْرِ

زَكَاةُ الْفِطْرِ وَاجِبَةٌ عَلَى كُلِّ مُسْلِمٍ، الذَّكَرُ وَالأُنْثَى، وَالصَّغِيرُ وَالْكَبِيرُ، وَالْعَبْدُ وَالْحُرُّ.

عَنِ ابْنِ عُمَرَ رَضِيَ اللهُ عَنْهُمَا قَالَ: ((فَرَضَ رَسُولُ اللهِ صلى الله عليه وسلم - زَكَاةَ الْفِطْرِ صَاعًا مِنْ تَمْرٍ، أَوْ صَاعًا مِنْ شَعِيرٍ، عَلَى الْعَبْدِ وَالْحُرِّ وَالذَّكَرِ وَالأُنْثَى، وَالصَّغِيرِ وَالْكَبِيرِ، مِنَ الْمُسْلِمِينَ، وَأَمَرَ بِهَا أَنْ تُؤَدَّى قَبْلَ خُرُوجِ النَّاسِ إِلَى الصَّلاَةِ)) [رَوَاهُ البُخَارِي وَمُسْلِم].

أَجَازَ الْعُلَمَاءُ إِخْرَاجَ زَكَاةِ الْفِطْرِ قَبْلَ الْعِيدِ بِيَوْمٍ أَوْ يَوْمَيْنِ، وَلاَ يَجُوزُ تَأْخِيرُهَا إِلَى مَا بَعْدَ صَلاَةِ الْعِيدِ.

Zakatul-Fitr (fast-breaking charity) is obligatory on every Muslim, young or old, and male or female.

Ibn Umar reported that: "Allah's Messenger, peace be upon him, has ordained to pay Zakatul-Fitr, one Sa'a (it is a unit of measurement) of dates or barley on every Muslim slave or free, male or female, young or old. And he ordered to be paid before the Eid prayer." [Al-Bukhari and Muslim].

The scholars said: it is permitted to give it one or two days before Eid, and it is not allowed to delay it after Eid Prayer.

تَعْرِيفُ الصَّاع:

الصَّاعُ يُعَادِلُ أَرْبَعَ حَفْنَاتٍ بِالْيَدَيْنِ الْمُعْتَدِلَتَيْنِ الْمُمْتَلِئَتَيْنِ، وَمِقْدَارُهُ بِالْوَزْنِ يَخْتَلِفُ بِاخْتِلَافِ نَوْعِ الطَّعَام.

Definition: One Sa'a is equivalent to full four moderate hands. Its weight depends on the kind of food (It is estimated between 2.6 kilograms to 3.0 kilograms).

Fasting – الصِّيَامُ

الصَّوْمُ أحَدُ أرْكَانِ الإسْلامِ الْخَمْسَةِ، وَمَنْزِلَتُهُ عِنْدَ اللهِ عَظِيمَةٌ، وَفَضَائِلُهُ كَثِيرَةٌ، وَقَدْ فَرَضَ اللهُ صِيَامَ شَهْرِ رَمَضَانَ مِنْ كُلِّ عَامٍ عَلَى كُلِّ مُسْلِمٍ بَالِغٍ عَاقِلٍ مُقِيمٍ قَادِرٍ عَلَى الصِّيَام.

قَالَ تَعَالَى: ﴿يَا أَيُّهَا الَّذِينَ آمَنُوا كُتِبَ عَلَيْكُمُ الصِّيَامُ كَمَا كُتِبَ عَلَى الَّذِينَ مِن قَبْلِكُمْ لَعَلَّكُمْ تَتَّقُونَ * أَيَّامًا مَّعْدُودَاتٍ ۚ فَمَن كَانَ مِنكُم مَّرِيضًا أَوْ عَلَىٰ سَفَرٍ فَعِدَّةٌ مِّنْ أَيَّامٍ أُخَرَ﴾ [البَقَرة: 183-184].

وَقَالَ ﷺ: ((بُنِيَ الإسْلَامُ عَلَى خَمْسٍ: شَهَادَةِ أَنْ لَا إِلَـهَ إِلَّا اللهُ، وَأَنَّ مُحَمَّـدًا، رَسُولُ اللهِ، وَإِقَامِ الصَّلَاةِ، وَإِيتَاءِ الزَّكَاةِ، وَحَجِّ الْبَيْتِ، وَصَوْمِ رَمَضَانَ)) [رَواهُ البُخارِي ومُسْلِم].

Fasting is one of the five main pillars of Islam and has many virtues. Allah has prescribed fasting the month of Ramadan every year on every Muslim who is an adult, sane, resident and able to fast. Allah Almighty said: "O you who believe! The fasting is prescribed for you as was prescribed for those before you, that you may attain piety (fearing of Allah)* Observing fasting for a fixed number of days, but if any of you is ill or on a journey, then fast other days (after Ramadan)." [2: 183-184].

And the Prophet, peace be upon him, said: "Islam is built on five pillars: testifying that there is no god but Allah, Muhammad is the Messenger of Allah, performing the prayer, paying Zakah (obligatory charity), performing the pilgrimage to the House of Allah, and fasting the month of Ramadan." [Al-Bukhari and Muslim].

فَضَائِلُ وَسُنَنُ صِيَامِ شَهْرَ رَمَضَان
The Virtues of Fasting the Month of Ramadan

فَضَائِلُ صِيَامِ شَهْرِ رَمَضَانَ كَثِيرَةٌ ومُتَعَدِّدَةٌ مِنْهَا:

1. الصَّوْمُ عِبادَةٌ عَظِيمَةٌ وَهُوَ أحَـدُ أرْكَانِ الإسْلامِ.
2. صَوْمُ شَهْرِ رَمَضَانَ يُكَفِّرُ الذُّنُوب، قَالَ ﷺ: ((مَنْ صَامَ رَمَضَانَ إيمَانًا وَاحْتِسَابًا غُفِرَ لَهُ مَا تَقَدَّمَ مِنْ ذَنْبِهِ)) [رواه البُخاري].
3. الصَّوْمُ سَبَبٌ لِاسْتِجَابَةِ الدُّعَاءِ.
4. فِيهِ لَيْلَةٌ مُبارَكَةٌ، لَيْلَةُ القَدْرِ، وَهِيَ خَيْرٌ مِنْ ألْفِ شَهْرٍ، قَالَ تَعَالَى: ﴿لَيْلَةُ الْقَدْرِ خَيْرٌ مِنْ أَلْفِ شَهْرٍ﴾ [القَدر: 3].
5. فِيهِ تُفْتَحُ أبْوَابُ الجَنَّةِ، وَتُغْلَقُ أبْوَابُ جَهَنَّمَ، قَالَ ﷺ: ((إذَا دَخَلَ رَمَضَانُ فُتِّحَتْ أَبْوَابُ الْجَنَّةِ، وَغُلِّقَتْ أَبْوَابُ جَهَنَّمَ، وَسُلْسِلَتِ الشَّيَاطِينُ)) [البُخاري ومسلم].
6. أدَاءُ الْعُمْرَةِ فِي رَمَضَانَ تَعْدِلُ حَجَّةً (فِي الثَّوَابِ).
7. لِلصَّائِمِ فَرْحَتَانِ: قَالَ ﷺ: ((لِلصَّائِمِ فَرْحَتَانِ: فَرْحَةٌ عِنْدَ فِطْرِهِ، وَفَرْحَةٌ عِنْدَ لِقَاءِ رَبِّهِ)) [البُخاري ومسلم].

سُنَنِ الصِّيَامِ

1. صَلَاةُ التَّرَاوِيحِ لَهَا فَضْلٌ كَبِيرٌ، قَالَ ﷺ: ((مَنْ قَامَ رَمَضَانَ إيمَانًا وَاحْتِسَابًا، غُفِرَ لَهُ مَا تَقَدَّمَ مِنْ ذَنْبِهِ)) [البُخاري وَمُسْلِم].
2. تَعْجِيلُ الإفْطَارِ وَالأفْضَلُ أنْ يَكُونَ عَلَى تَمْرٍ أوْ مَاءٍ.
3. تَأْخِيرُ السُّحُورِ فِيهِ خَيْرٌ وَبَرَكَةٌ.
4. الدُّعَاءُ قَبْلَ وَعِنْدَ الْإفْطَارِ مِنْ مَوَاطِنِ إجَابَةِ الدُّعَاءِ.
5. الإِكْثَارُ مِنْ قِرَاءَةِ الْقُرْآنِ وَالْإعْتِكَافُ فِي الْعَشْرِ الْأوَاخِرِ.

The Virtues of Fasting the Month of Ramadan

1. Fasting is a worship and has a great reward from the almighty Allah.
2. Fasting is the expiation for sins. The Prophet, peace be upon him, said: "Whoever fasted the month of Ramadan out of faith and hope of reward from Allah, then all his past sins forgiven." [Al-Bukhari].
3. Fasting is a reason for responding to the supplication.
4. The night of Al-Qadr, the blessing night is better than a thousand months. It is in Ramadan.
5. In Ramadan the gates of Heaven are opened, the gates of Hell are closed, and the devils are chained.
6. Performance of Umra in Ramadan is equivalent to Hajj (in reward).
7. The Messenger of Allah said: "There are two joys for the fasting person: One joy when he breaks his fast, and the other joy when he meets his Lord." [Al-Bukhari and Muslim].

Some Great Deeds:

1. Taraweeh prayer has great virtues. The Prophet, peace be upon him said: "Whoever prayed, Taraweeh, at night during Ramadan out of faith and hope of reward from Allah, all his past sins will be forgiven." [Al-Bukhari and Muslim].
2. It is best speeding up breakfast and have dates or water.
3. Delaying Suhor is good and blessing.
4. It is recommended to make supplication at breakfast.
5. Reciting the Qur'an has a great reward. Ramadan is the month of the Qur'an, and Itikaf (seclusion at Masjid) in the last ten days of Ramadan.

Voluntary Fasting - صِيَامُ التَّطَوُّع

الصِّيَامُ عِبَادَةٌ عَظِيمَةٌ وَفِيهِ أجْرٌ كَبِيرٌ، وَقَدْ بَيَّنَ الرَّسُولُ، صلى الله عليه وسلم، اِسْتِحْبَابَ صِيَام أيَّامٍ مُعَيَّنَةٍ، وَمِنْ هَذِهِ الأيَّام:

1- صِيَامُ يَوْمِ الإثْنَيْنِ وَالْخَمِيسِ.

2- صِيَامُ ثَلَاثَةِ أيَّامٍ مِنْ كُلِّ شَهْرٍ، وَالْأفْضَلُ صِيَام الأيّام الْبِيض (يَوْم 13، وَ 14، وَ 15 مِنْ كُلِّ شَهْرٍ هِجْرِي).

3- صِيَامُ سِتَّةِ أيَّامٍ مِنْ شَوَّال (مُتَفَرِّقَةً أَوْ مُتَتَابِعَةً).

4- صِيَامُ يَوْمِ عَرَفَةَ لِغَيرِ الْحَاجّ (الْيَوْمُ التَّاسِعُ مِنْ ذِي الْحِجَّة).

5- صِيَامُ يَوْمِ عَاشُورَاء (الْيَوْمُ الْعَاشِرُ مِنْ مُحَرّم) وَالْأفْضَلُ أَنْ يَصُومَ يَوْمًا قَبْلَهُ أَوْ يَوْمًا بَعْدَهُ.

6- صِيَامُ يَوْمٍ وَإفْطَارُ يَوْمٍ (صِيَام دَاوُد عَلَيْهِ السَّلَام).

Fasting is a great worship and has a great reward from Allah. The Prophet, peace is upon him, specified certain days to fast, that has more reward from Allah, and these days are:

1. Fasting on Mondays and Thursdays.

2. Fasting three days of each month (And best to fast are the 13th , 14th, and 15th days of each Hijri month).

3. Fasting six days of Shawwal (separate or consecutive).

4. Fasting on the day of Arafah (9th day of dul-Hijjah), for the one who is not at the Pilgrimage.

5. Fasting on the Day of Ashura (the 10th day of Muharam) and it is better to fast one day before it or one day after it.

6. Fasting one day and breakfast one day (This is the fasting of Daud (David), peace be upon him).

Hajj - الْحَجُّ

الْحَجُّ أَحَدُ أَرْكَانِ الإِسْلامِ الْخَمْسَةِ، وَهُوَ فَرْضُ عَيْنٍ عَلَى كُلِّ مُسْلِمٍ بَالِغٍ عاقِلٍ مُسْتَطِيعٍ (يَمْلِكُ الزَّادَ وَالرَّاحِلَةَ وَأَمْنَ الطَّرِيقِ إِلَى بَيْتِ اللهِ الْحَرَامِ) مَرَّةً وَاحِدَةً فِي العُمْرِ. قَالَ تَعَالَى: ﴿وَللهِ عَلَى النَّاسِ حِجُّ الْبَيْتِ مَنِ اسْتَطَاعَ إِلَيْهِ سَبِيلاً﴾ [آلِ عِمران: 97].

وَقَالَ صلى الله عليه وسلم: ((يَا أَيُّهَا النَّاسُ، قَدْ فَرَضَ اللهُ عَلَيْكم الحَجَّ فحُجُّوا)) [مُسْلِم].

Hajj (Pilgrimage to Makkah) **is one of the five pillars of Islam**. Hajj is obligated by Allah on every Muslim, who is an adult and mindful and capable (has a provision, transportation, and the road to Makkah is saved) once in a lifetime. Allah Most High said: “It is the duty of all people towards Allah to do Pilgrimage to the House of Allah, if they have the means and ability to do it.” [3: 97]. Also the Prophet, peace be upon him, said: “O people, Allah have imposed Hajj on you, so do it.” [Muslim].

Pillars of Hajj - أَرْكَانُ الْحَجّ

أَرْكَانُ الْحَجِّ أَرْبَعَة وَلَا يَصِحُّ الْحَجُّ إِلَّا بِهَا وَهِيَ:

1- الْإِحْرَامُ بِالحَجِّ مِنَ المِيقَات: وَهُوَ نِيَّةُ الدُّخُولِ فِي النُّسكِ، ويُستَحَبُّ الإغْتِسَالُ قَبْلَ الْإِحْرَامِ ثُمَّ لبسُ مَلَابِسِ الْإِحْرَامِ.

2- الْوُقُوفُ بِعَرَفَةَ: فِي الْيَوْمِ التَّاسِعِ مِنْ شَهْرِ ذِي الْحِجَّةِ، وَهُوَ مِنْ أَهَمِّ أَعْمَالِ الْحَجِّ، لِقَوْلِهِ صلى الله عليه وسلم: (الْحَجُّ عَرَفَةٌ) [التِّرمذي].

3- طَوافُ الإفَاضَةِ (الْبعْضُ يُسَمِّيهِ طَوافُ الزِّيارَةِ)**:** لِقَوْلِهِ تَعالى: ﴿وَلْيَطَّوَّفُوا بِالْبَيْتِ الْعَتِيقِ﴾ [الحجّ: 29]، وَالطَّوافُ عِبارَة عَنْ سَبْعَةِ أشْواطٍ حَوْلَ الكَعْبَة (اِجْعَلِ الْكَعْبَةَ عَنْ يَسارِكَ عِنْدَ الطَّوافِ).

4- السَّعْيُ بَيْنَ الصَّفَا وَالْمَرْوَة لِقَوْلِه ﷺ: ((اِسْعَوْا فَإِنَّ اللهَ كَتَبَ عَلَيْكُمُ السَّعْيَ)) [رَواهُ أحْمد].

The pillars of Hajj are four, and the Hajj is valid only by doing all of them.

1. Al-Ihram: It is the intention to enter the acts of Hajj, and it is Sunnah taking a shower before wearing the Ihram clothes.

2. Standing at Arafah: On the ninth day of Dhul-Hijjah, all pilgrims go to Arafah. Standing in Arafah is one of the most important acts of Hajj, the Prophet, peace be upon him, said: "Hajj is Arafah." [al-Tirmidhi].

3. Tawaaf al-Efathah: To go around the Kaaba seven times.

4. Sa'y is walking between Safa and Marwah: Waking seven times between Safa and Marwah (walking from Safa to Marwah counted one time and waking from Marwah to Safa counted another time). The Prophet, peace be upon him, said: "Seek between Safa and Marwah, certainly, Allah has written for you to seek." [Ahmad].

♦ **أَشْهُرُ الْحَجِّ:** شَوَّالٌ، وَذُو الْقَعْدَةِ، وَذُو الْحِجَّةِ.

♦ **Months of the Hajj are:**
Shawwal, Dhu'l-Qa'da and Dhu'l-Hijjah.

The Duties of Hajj – وَجِبَاتُ الحَجِّ

لِلْحَجِّ وَاجِبَاتٌ مِنْهَا:

1- الإِحْرَامُ مِنَ الْمِيقَاتِ.

2- الْوُقُوفُ بِعَرَفَةَ إِلَى غُرُوبِ الشَّمْسِ.

3- الْمَبِيتُ بِمُزْدَلِفَةَ.

4- الْمَبِيتُ بِمِنَى لَيَالِي التَّشْرِيقِ.

5- رَمْيُ الْجَمَرَاتِ بِالتَّرْتِيبِ.

6- الْحَلْقُ أَوْ التَّقْصِيرُ لِلتَّحَلُّلِ مِنَ الإِحْرَامِ.

7- طَوَافُ الْوَدَاعِ (سَبْعَةُ أَشْوَاطٍ حَوْلَ الْكَعْبَةِ) قَبْلَ السَّفَرِ.

إِذَا كَانَ الحَاجّ مُتَمَتِعًا أَوْ قَارِنًا فَعَلَيْهِ هَدْي وَاجِب (ذَبْح شَاة)

Duties of Hajj are:

1. Starting the Ihram from the Meeqaat.

2. Standing at Arafah from the sunrise on the ninth day of Dual-Hijjah until sunset.

3. Sleeping overnight in Muzdalifah.

4. Sleeping overnight in Mina on the nights of Tashreeq.

5. Throwing the Jamarat (stones) in order.

6. Cutting the hair or shortening it to designate from Ihram.

7. Farewell Tawaf (go around the Kaaba seven times).

* Sacrifice is obligatory if the Haj is Mutamattia or Qiran

وَاجِبَاتُ الْحَجِّ تَنْجَبِرُ بِالدَّمِ – ذَبْحُ شَاةٍ – وَالْحَجُّ صَحِيحٌ

Hajj is valid in the absence of one of the duties, but the person (Hajj) must slaughter a sheep to make it up.

Virtues of Hajj - فَضَائِلُ الحَجِّ

لِلْحَجِّ فَضَائِلُ كَثِيرَةٌ مِنْهَا:

1. الْحَجُّ سَبَبٌ لِنَفْيِ الفَقْرِ وَالذُّنُوبِ، قَالَ ﷺ: ((تَابِعُوا بَيْنَ الْحَجِّ وَالْعُمْرَةِ فَإِنَّهُمَا يَنْفِيَانِ الْفَقْرَ وَالذُّنُوبَ)) [صَحِيح سُنن التِّرمذي].

2. الْحَجُّ سَبَبٌ لِلْعِتْقِ مِنَ النَّارِ فَفِي الْحَدِيثِ ((مَا مِنْ يَوْمٍ أَكْثَرَ مِنْ أَنْ يُعْتِقَ اللهُ فِيهِ عَبْدًا مِنَ النَّارِ مِنْ يَوْمِ عَرَفَةَ)) [مُسْلِم].

3. الْحَجُّ سَبَبٌ لِدُخُولِ الجَنَّةِ، قَالَ ﷺ: ((الْحَجُّ الْمَبْرُور لَيْسَ لَهُ جَزَاء إِلَّا الجَنَّة)) [البُخَارِي].

4. الْحَجُّ تَعْظِيمٌ لِشَعَائِرِ اللهِ، قَالَ تَعَالَى: ﴿ ذَٰلِكَ وَمَن يُعَظِّمْ شَعَٰٓئِرَ ٱللَّهِ فَإِنَّهَا مِن تَقْوَى﴾ [الحَجّ: 32].

1-The Hajj is a reason for the denial of poverty and sins. The Prophet, peace be upon him, said: "Follow the Hajj and Umrah, they deny poverty and sins." [At-Tirmidhi].

2-The Hajj is a reason to be saved from the fire. The Prophet, peace be upon him, said: "There is no day more than that Allah will take slaves from the fire than from the Day of Arafah." [Muslim].

3-The Hajj is a reason for entering paradise, in the Hadith: "The accepted Hajj has no reward except Paradise." [Bukhari].

4-The Hajj is glorifying the commands of Allah. Allah said: "That is. And whosoever respects the Symbols of Allah, then it is truly coming from purity of heart." [22: 32]

قَالَ الْعُلَمَاءُ: حَجُّ الصَّبِيِّ صَحِيحٌ، وَلَكِنْ لَا يَجْزِيهِ عَنْ حَجَّةِ الإِسْلَامِ

The scholars said: The child is rewarded for his Hajj, but not counted as an obligatory Hajj.

Umrah - العُمْـرَةُ

الْعُمْرَةُ سُنَّةٌ مُؤَكَّدَةٌ وَيَرَى بَعْضُ الْعُلَمَاءِ أَنَّهَا وَاجِبَةٌ لِقَوْلِهِ تَعَالَى: ﴿وَأَتِمُّوا الْحَجَّ وَالْعُمْرَةَ لِلَّهِ﴾ [البَقَرَة: 196].

أَرْكَانُ الْعُمْرَةِ ثَلَاثَةٌ: Pillars of Umrah are three

1- **الإِحْرَامُ** (نِيَّةُ الدُّخُولِ فِي النُّسُكِ) مِنَ المِيقَاتِ.

2 - **الطَّوَافُ** بِالْكَعْبَةِ سَبْعَةُ أَشْوَاطٍ (اِجْعَلِ الْكَعْبَةَ عَنْ يَسَارِكَ).

3 - **السَّعْيُ بَيْنَ الصَّفَا وَالْمَرْوَةِ** سَبْعَةُ أَشْوَاطٍ (مِنَ الصَّفَا إِلَى الْمَرْوَةِ شَوْطٌ وَالرُّجُوعِ إِلَى الصَّفَا شَوْطٌ آخَرُ).

♦ **وَقْتُ أَدَاءِ الْعُمْرَةِ:** يُمْكِنُ أَدَاءُ الْعُمْرَةِ فِي أَيِّ وَقْتٍ مِنَ السَّنَةِ، وَأَفْضَلُ وَقْتٍ لِفِعْلِهَا فِي شَهْرِ رَمَضَانَ.

Umrah is a recommended Sunnah, and some scholars said: It is obligatory because Allah said: "And complete Hajj and Umrah for Allah." [2: 196].

Umrah has three pillars:

1- Ihram (Intention to start the action of Hajj) from the Meeqaat (Known certain places).

2-Tawaaf around the Kaaba seven times (make the Kaaba on your left hand when you are making Tawaaf).

3- Sa'y is waking between Safa and Marwa seven times (from Safa to Marwa one count, and returning to Safa, another count).

♦ **Time of performing Umrah:** Umrah can be performed at any time of the year, and the best time is to do it in the month of Ramadan.

دُرُوسٌ مِنَ السِّيرَةِ وَالتَّارِيخ

Lessons from Biography and History

قَالَ اللهُ تَعَالَى:

﴿لَقَدْ كَانَ لَكُمْ فِي رَسُولِ اللهِ أُسْوَةٌ حَسَنَةٌ﴾

"There has certainly been for you in the Messenger of Allah an excellent example."

[33: 21] [الأحْزَاب: 21]

حَالُ العَرَبِ قَبْلَ الإسْلامِ
The Life of Arabs before Islam

كَانَتِ الجَزِيرَةُ العَرَبِيَّة فِي جَاهِلِيَّةٍ مُظْلِمَةٍ، قَبْلَ الإسْلامِ. كَانَ يَعُمُّهَا الجَهْلُ والظّلْمُ وَكَثْرَةُ الحُرُوبِ لِأَتْفَهِ الأسْبَابِ والتّعَصُّب لِلْقبِيلَةِ.
اِنْتَشَرَ بيْنَ النَّاسِ التَّعَامُلُ بِالرِّبَا، وَشُرْبُ الخَمْرِ، وَوَأْدُ البَنَاتِ، وَلِهَذِهِ الأسْبَاب وَغَيْرِهَا لَمْ يَسْتَطِعْ أحَدٌ مِنَ زُعَمَاءِ العَرَب أَنْ يُوَحِّدَ هَذِهِ القَبائِلَ المُتفَرِّقَةِ المُتنَاحِرَةِ.
كَانَ أَغْلَبُ السُكّانِ يَعْبُدُونَ الأوْثَانَ وَالأصْنَامَ، وَقَلِيلٌ مِنْهُم كَانُوا عَلَى مِلَّةِ ابْرَاهِيم، عَلَيْهِ السَّلَام، وَلَكِنْ رَغْمَ الجَهْلِ وَالظُّلمِ كَانَ لِلْعَرَبِ بَعْضُ العَادَاتِ الحَمِيدَةِ، مِثْلِ الشَّجَاعَةِ وَالكَرَمِ وَالوَفَاءِ بِالعَهْدِ وَالوَعْدِ، وَكَانُوا يُعَظِّمُونَ الكَعْبَةَ وَيَحُجُّونَ إلَيْهَا، وَيَقُولُونَ إنَّ لِلْبَيْتِ رَبٌّ يَحْمِيهِ، وَكَانُوا يُحِبُّونَ الشِّعْرَ وَالخَطَابَةَ.

The Arabs in the Arabian Peninsula, before Islam, lived as nomads. Their lives were permeated by ignorance, injustice, and intolerance. Many wars happened between them for simple reasons. The actions of evil and sin spread among them, such as dealing with interest, killing the girls, and drinking alcohol. For these and other reasons, none of the Arab leaders could unite these scattered and competing tribes. The Arabs were worshiping idols, believing they can harm them or benefit them. However, there were a few Arabs on the religion of Abraham - peace be upon him - they respected the Kaabah and believed a God was protecting it. Despite the spread of ignorance and injustice, the Arabs had some good habits and virtues, such as courage, generosity, and fulfillment of the promise. Also, they loved poetry, rhetoric, and public speaking.

مَوْلِدُ وَنَسَبُ النَّبِيّ ﷺ
The Prophet's Birth and Descent

◆- **النَّبِيُّ**، ﷺ، أفْضَلُ العَرَبِ نَسَبًا، وَحَسَبًا، وَشَرَفًا، وَهُوَ مِنْ قَبِيلَةِ قُرَيْشٍ، وَهِيَ أَفْضَلُ قَبَائِلِ الْعَرَب. وُلِدَ ﷺ، فِي مَكَّةَ، وَكَان ذَلِكَ يَوْم الإثْنَيْنِ مِنْ شَهْرِ رَبِيعِ الأوَّلِ، عَامَ الفِيلِ 570م.

◆- **وَالِدُهُ**: عَبْدُ اللهِ بْنُ عَبْدُ المُطَّلب بْنُ هَاشِم بْنُ عَبْدُ مَنَاف القُرَشِي ويَرْجِعُ نَسَبهُ إلَى إسْمَاعِيلَ بْنِ إبْرَاهِيمَ عَلَيْهِمَا السّلَام.

◆- **أُمُّهُ**: آمِنَة بِنْتُ وَهَبٍ بِنْتُ عَبْدُ مَنَاف.

◆- **مُرْضِعَتُهُ**: حَلِيمَةُ السَّعْدِيّةُ وَقَدْ مَكَثَ عِنْدَهَا خَمْسَ سَنَوَاتٍ.

◆- **عَاشَ النَّبِيُّ** ﷺ، يَتِيمًا، إذْ مَاتَ أبُوهُ، عَبدُ اللهِ، قَبْلَ وِلَادَتِهِ، وَمَاتَتْ أُمُّهُ، آمِنَةُ، وَعُمْرُهُ سِتُّ سَنَوَاتٍ، ثُمَّ مَاتَ جَدُّهُ، عَبْدُ المُطَّلبِ، وَعُمْرُهُ ثَمَانِي سَنَوَاتٍ فَكَفَلَهُ عَمُّهُ أبُوطَالِب.

◆- **أسْمَاءُ النَّبِيِّ** ﷺ: مُحَمَّدٌ، وَأَحْمَدُ، وَالْحَاشِرُ، وَالْمَاحِي، وَالْعَاقِبُ. قَالَ ﷺ: ((لِي خَمْسَةُ أَسْمَاءٍ: أَنَا مُحَمَّدٌ، وَأَحْمَدُ، وَأَنَا الْمَاحِي الَّذِي يَمْحُو اللهُ بِيَ الْكُفْرَ، وَأَنَا الْحَاشِرُ الَّذِي يُحْشَرُ النَّاسُ عَلَى قَدَمِي، وَأَنَا الْعَاقِبُ)) [البُخارِي وَمُسْلِم].

◆- **كُنْيَتُهُ** ﷺ: كَانَ النَّبِيُّ، ﷺ، يُكْنَى أَبَا القَاسِم، وَكَانَ القَاسِمُ أكْبَرَ أوْلَادِهِ مِنْ زَوْجَتِهِ خَدِيجَةَ، رَضِيَ اللهُ عَنْهَا.

◆- **تُوُفِّيَ** ﷺ، يَوْمَ الإثْنَيْنِ، الثَّانِيَ عَشَرَ مِنْ شَهْرِ رَبِيعِ الأوَّلِ مِنَ السَّنةِ الحَادِيَة عَشْرَةَ لِلْهِجْرَةِ، وَكَانَ لَهُ مِنَ العُمَر 63 عَامًا.

The Prophet's Birth and Descent

♦ - **The Prophet, Muhammad,** peace be upon him, was from the best and noblest Arab family, from the Quraysh tribe. He was born in Makkah on Monday, 570 A.D.

♦ - **His father:** Abdullah ibn Abdul-Muttalib ibn Hashem ibn Abdu-Manaf al-Qureshi, which related to Ismail ibn Ibrahim peace be upon them. The Prophet, peace be upon him, was born in the best noble Arab family.

♦ - **His mother:** Amina bint Wahab bin Abdu-Manaf.

♦ - **His Nurse:** Halima Al-Saadiyah. He stayed with her for about five years.

♦ - **The Prophet, peace be upon him, lived as an orphan**. His father died before his birth, his mother died when he was six years old, and his grandfather, Abdul-Mutallab, died when he was eight years old, so his uncle Abu-Talib became his guardian.

♦ - **Names of the Prophet**: The Prophet, peace be upon him, said: "I have five names: I am Muhammad, I am Ahmad, I am Al-Mahi (whom Allah by him wipes disbelief), I am Al-Hasir (the one whom the people gathered at his feet), and I am Al-Aqib (the one after whom there is no Prophet)." [Bukhari and Muslim].

♦ - **His nickname**: The nickname of the Prophet, peace be upon him, was Abul-Qasim, and Al-Qasim was his oldest son from his wife Khadija, may Allah be pleased with her.

♦ - **He passed away** on Monday, 3/12/11H. He was 63 years old.

حَياةُ النَّبيِّ ﷺ قَبْلَ الْبِعْثَةِ
The Prophet's Life before the Mission

عَاشَ النَّبيُّ، مُحَمَّدٌ، ﷺ، فِي قَبِيلَتِهِ قُرَيْشٍ أرْبَعِينَ عَاماً قَبْلَ النُّبُوَّةِ، وَكَانَ فِيهَا مِثَالًا لِلْخُلقِ الْحَسَنِ فِي التَّعَامُلِ مَعَ النّاسِ، حَتَّى أَنَّهُم لَقَّبُوهُ بِالصَّادِقِ الأَمِينِ. كَانَ رَسُولُ اللهِ، ﷺ، قَبْلَ الإسْلَامِ يَعْبُدُ اللهَ عَلى مِلَّةِ إبْراهِيمَ وَيَرْفُضُ عِبَادَةَ الأوْثَانِ. كَانَ ﷺ، يَذْهَبُ إِلَى غَارِ حِرَاءِ، لِيَخْلُوَ بِنَفْسِهِ وَيَتَعَبَّدَ اللهَ.

فِي صِغَرِهِ ﷺ، عَمِلَ بِالرَّعْيِ ثُمَّ عَمِلَ بِالتِّجَارَةِ لِخَدِيجَةَ بِنْتُ خُوَيْلِد، وَكَانَتْ ذَاتَ شَرَفٍ وَثَرَاءٍ. عَلِمَتْ خَدِيجَةُ، رَضِيَ اللهُ عَنْهَا، مِنْ خَادِمِهَا مَيْسَرَةَ عَنْ خُلُقِ النَّبِيِّ، وَحُسْنِ مُعَامَلَتِهِ وَأَمَانَتِهِ، فَعَرَضَتْ عَلَيْهِ أَنْ يَتَزَوَّجَهَا فَوَافَقَ النَّبِيُّ، ﷺ، عَلَى ذَلِكَ وَكَانَ عُمْرُهُ آنَذَاكَ خَمْسَ وَعِشْرِينَ سَنَةٍ. وُلِدَتْ خَدِيجَةُ لِرَسُولِ اللهِ، ﷺ، جَمِيعَ وَلَدِهِ إِلَّا إِبْرَاهِيمَ فَإِنَّهُ مِنْ مَارِيَةَ القُبْطِيَّةَ.

كَانَ ﷺ يُحِبُّ خَدِيجَةَ كَثِيرًا، وَتَكْرِيمًا لَهَا لَمْ يَتَزَوَّجْ عَلَيْهَا حَتَّى مَاتَتْ، رَضِيَ اللهُ عَنْهَا.

The Prophet Muhammad, peace be upon him, lived with his tribe – Quraysh (in Makkah) – for forty years, before he became a Prophet. He was honest and dealt with people nicely. So they called him, "the truthful and the trustworthy." He was on the religion of Abraham before Islam. He never worshipped idols. The Prophet, peace be upon him, used to go to the cave of Hira, which was away from people. He devoted himself to worship Allah Almighty. In his early life, he worked on taking care of sheep, and then he worked in the trade for a noble and rich woman named Khadijah bent Quailed. Khadijah learned about the good manners and honesty of the Prophet, peace be upon him, from her servant, Maisara. Therefore, she proposed to marry him, and he accepted her. He was 25 years old when he married Khadijah. All of his children were from her, except for his son Ibrahim, who was from Maria Coptic. The Prophet Muhammad, peace be upon him, loved Khadijah, and honored her. He did not marry other women until she died, may Allah be pleased with her.

بِعْثَةُ النَّبِيِّ صلى الله عليه وسلم
The Mission of the Prophet

كَانَ النَّبِيُّ صلى الله عليه وسلم، قَبْلَ البِعْثَةِ يَذْهَبُ إِلَى غَارِ حِرَاءِ فِي جَبَلِ النُّورِ لِلْعِبَادَةِ وَالتَّفَكُّرِ فِي مَخْلُوقَاتِ اللهِ. لَمَّا بَلَغَ النَّبِيُّ صلى الله عليه وسلم، الأَرْبَعِينَ مِنْ عُمْرِهِ نَزَلَ عَلَيْهِ جِبْرِيل، عَلَيْهِ السَّلَام، وَهُوَ فِي الغَارِ وَكَانَ ذَلِكَ فِي شَهْرِ رَمَضَانَ، وَقَالَ لَهُ: إِقْرَأ، قَالَ: صلى الله عليه وسلم، مَا أَنَا بِقَارِئٍ، فَأَعَادَ عَلَيْهِ ذَلِكَ ثَلَاثًا، ثُمَّ قَالَ لَهُ: ﴿اقْرَأْ بِاسْمِ رَبِّكَ الَّذِي خَلَقَ * خَلَقَ الْإِنْسَانَ مِنْ عَلَقٍ﴾ [العلق: 1-2]. رَجَعَ صلى الله عليه وسلم، إِلَى بَيْتِهِ وَأَخْبَرَ زَوْجَتَهُ، خَدِيجَةَ، بِمَا حَدَثَ لَهُ فَهَدَّأَتْهُ وَبَشَّرَتْهُ بِالخَيْرِ وَقَالَتْ وَاللهِ مَا يُخْزِيكَ اللهُ أَبَدًا، إِنَّكَ لَتَصِلُ الرَّحِمَ، وَتَقْرِي الضَّيْفَ، وَتُعِينُ عَلَى نَوَائِبِ الحَقِّ. ذَهَبَتْ السَّيِّدَةُ خَدِيجَةُ إِلَى وَرَقَةِ ابْنِ نُوفَلَ – ابْنُ عَمِّهَا – وَكَانَ عِنْدَهُ عِلْمٌ بِالتَّوْرَاةِ وَالإِنْجِيلِ وَقِصَصِ الأَنْبِيَاءِ، فَأَخْبَرَتْهُ بِمَا حَدَثَ لِلرَّسُولِ فِي الغَارِ فَطَمْأَنَهَا وَقَالَ لَهَا لَقَدْ جَاءَهُ النَّامُوسُ الأَكْبَرُ الَّذِي كَانَ يَأْتِي لِمُوسَى، وَإِنَّهُ لَنَبِيُّ هَذِهِ الأُمَّةِ.

بَعْدَ فَتْرَةٍ مِنَ الزَّمَن نَزَلَ عَلَيْهِ قَوْلُ اللهِ تَعَالَى: ﴿ يَا أَيُّهَا الْمُدَّثِّرُ * قُمْ فَأَنْذِرْ * وَرَبَّكَ فَكَبِّرْ ﴾ [المدثر: 1-3]، فَقَامَ ﷺ، يَدْعُو النَّاسَ إِلَى الإِسْلَامِ سِرًا لِمُدَّةِ ثَلَاثِ سِنِينَ، وَبَعْدَهَا جَهَرَ بِدَعْوَتِهِ وَأَخَذَ يَدْعُو النَّاسَ إِلَى عِبَادَةِ اللهِ وَتَرْكِ عِبَادَةِ الأَصْنَامِ. مَكَثَ ﷺ، بِمَكَّةَ ثَلَاثَ عَشْرَةَ سَنَةً وأقام بِالْمَدِينَةِ بَعْدَ الهِجْرَةِ عَشْرَ سِنِينَ، وَمَاتَ وَهُوَ ابْنُ ثَلَاثٍ وَسِتِّينَ سَنَةً – صَلَّى اللهُ عَلَيْهِ وَسَلَّم.

The Mission of the Prophet

Before his mission, the Prophet, peace be upon him, used to go to Hira Cave in the Noor Mountain. He would go there to worship and think about the creation of Allah. When the Prophet reached the age of forty years old, Gabriel, peace bc upon him, came to him while he was in the cave. This event was during the month of Ramadan. The Angel Gabriel said to him: “Read.” He, peace be upon him, said: “I am not a reader. ” Gabriel then repeated the question three times and said: “Read in the name of your Lord Who Created (everything)* He Created man from a clot.” [96: 1-2]. He, peace be upon him, read and then returned to his home and told his wife, Khadijah, what happened to him. She calmed him down and said: “Allah will not betray you, you connect the enjoins ties of kinship, you welcome guests, and you help people when they are in hardship.” Khadija went to her cousin, Warqa ibn Naufal, who knew the Torah and the Gospel and the stories of the previous prophets. After Khadija told him what happened to the Prophet, peace be upon him, in the cave, Waraqa said: “What has come to him is what has come to Moses, and he (Muhammad) is the Prophet of this nation.” After some time, Allah revealed to the Prophet: “O you (Muhammad) who covers himself . Arise and warn . And glorify your Lord" [15: 94], then he ﷺ, started calling people to Islam secretly for three years, after that he started publicly inviting people to worship Allah alone. He, ﷺ, stayed in Makkah for thirteen years and he lived in Madinah for ten years and he died when he was sixty-three years old.

مُحَمَّدٌ رَسُولُ الله ﷺ

Muhammad is the Messenger of Allah

♦ خَاتَمُ الأَنْبِيَاءِ وَالْمُرْسَلِين

He is the seal of Prophets and Messengers.

قَالَ تَعَالَى: ﴿مَّا كَانَ مُحَمَّدٌ أَبَا أَحَدٍ مِّن رِّجَالِكُمْ وَلَكِن رَّسُولَ اللهِ وَخَاتَمَ النَّبِيِّينَ﴾ [الأحزاب: 40].

Allah said: "Muhammad is not the father of any one of your men, but he is the Messenger of Allah and the Seal of the Prophets." [33:40].

♦- بُعِثَ إِلَى النَّاسِ كَافَّة

He is sent to all man kind

قَالَ تَعَالَى: ﴿ قُلْ يَٰٓأَيُّهَا ٱلنَّاسُ إِنِّى رَسُولُ ٱللَّهِ إِلَيْكُمْ جَمِيعًا ﴾ [الأعراف: 158].

Allah said: "O (Muhammad) say: O! Mankind! Verily, I am the Messenger of Allah, sent to you all." [7: 158].

♦- بُعِثَ رَحْمَةً لِلْعَالَمِين

He is Mercy to the Worlds

قَالَ تَعَالَى: ﴿ وَمَآ أَرْسَلْنَٰكَ إِلَّا رَحْمَةً لِّلْعَٰلَمِينَ ﴾ [الأنبياء: 107]

Allah said: "We have sent you (O Muhammad) not, but as a mercy to all the worlds." [21:107]

Migration to Abyssinia - الْهِجْرَةُ إِلَى الْحَبَشَةِ

اِشْتَدَّ الْأَذَى، وَالتَّعْذِيبُ وَالْإِضْطِهَادُ وَالتَّنْكِيلُ بِالْمُسْلِمِين عَلَى يَدِ الْمُشْرِكِينَ مِنْ قُرَيْشٍ، وَلِهَذَا أَمَرَ النَّبِيُّ ﷺ، أَصْحَابَهُ بِالْهِجْرَةِ إِلَى الْحَبَشَةِ وأَخْبَرَهُم بِأَنَّ بِهَا مَلِكًا عَادِلًا لَا يُظْلَمُ عِنْدَهُ أَحَد.

هَاجَرَ الْمُسْلِمُونَ إِلَى الْحَبَشَةِ فِرَارًا إِلَى اللهِ بِدِينِهِم وَخَوْفًا مِنَ الْفِتْنَةِ.

الْهِجْرَةُ الأولَى: فِي هَذِهِ الْهِجْرَةِ خَرَجَ أَحَدَ عَشَرَ رَجُلًا وَأَرْبَعُ نِسْوَةٍ سِرًّا وَكَانَ ذَلِكَ فِي شَهْرِ رَجَب سَنَة خَمْسَةٍ لِلْبِعْثَةِ، وَكَانَ أَوَّلُ مَنْ هَاجَرَ عُثْمَانُ بْنُ عَفَّان وَزَوْجَتُهُ رُقَيَّة (بِنْتُ النَّبِيِّ ﷺ).

الْهِجْرَةُ الثَّانِيَةُ: كَانَ عَدَدُ مَنْ خَرَجَ فِي الْهِجْرَةِ الثَّانِيَةِ ثَلَاثَةٌ وَثَمَانُونَ رَجُلًا وَتِسْعَ عَشْرَةَ اِمْرَأَةً بِقِيَادَةِ جَعْفَر بْنُ أَبِي طَالِب.

When the abuse and torture of Muslims by the polytheists of Quraysh intensified, the Prophet, peace be upon him, ordered his companions to migrate to Abyssinia (Ethiopia). He told them there is a just king there, and no one would be harmed or wronged in his kingdom. Muslims migrated to Abyssinia, for Allah's sake, to protect their life and religion.

First migration: In the month of Rajab, five years after the Prophet's mission, eleven men and four women secretly went out to Abyssinia. Uthman ibn Affan and his wife Rukia (the daughter of the Prophet), were the first to migrate.

Second migration: During the second migration, eighty-three men and nineteen women immigrated to Abyssinia. Jaafar ibn Abi Talib led them, may Allah be pleased with him.

Migration to Medina - الْهِجْرَةُ إِلَى الْمَدِينَةِ

اِزْدَادَ أذَى كُفَّارَ قُرَيْشٍ عَلَى المُسْلِمِينَ وَوَصَلَ بِهِم الأَمْر إِلَى الإِتِّفَاقِ عَلَى قَتْلِ النَّبِيِّ ﷺ.

عِنْدَمَا عَلِمَ النَّبِيُّ ﷺ، بِذَالِكَ أَمَرَ أَصْحَابَهُ بِالهِجْرَةِ إِلَى المَدِينَةِ، وَكَانَ نَفَرًا مِنْ أَهْلِ المَدِينَةِ قَدْ تَعَهَّدُوا عَلَى نُصْرَتِهِ إِذَا هَاجَر إِلَيهِمْ. بَدَأَ المُسْلِمُونَ فِي الهِجْرَةِ إِلَى المَدِينَةِ عَلَى شَكْلِ أَفْرَادٍ وَمَجْمُوعَاتٍ سِرًّا خَوْفًا مِنْ قُرَيْش، وَرُوِيَ أَنَّ عُمَرَ بْنُ الخَطَّاب، هَاجَرَ عَلَنًا وَتَحَدَّى قُرَيْشًا أَنْ تَعْتَرِضَ طَرِيقَه.

مَكَثَ النَّبِيُّ، ﷺ، بِمَكَّةَ حَتَّى أَذِنَ اللهُ لَهُ بِالهِجْرَةِ، فَأَخْبَرَ صَاحِبَهُ، أَبَابَكْرٍ، بِذَلِك. وَفِي لَيْلَةِ الهِجْرَةِ أَمَرَ النَّبِيُّ، ﷺ، عَلِيًّا، بِأَنْ يَبِيتَ عَلَى فِرَاشِهِ وَأَنْ يَنْتَظِرَ فِي مَكَّةَ حَتَّى يَرُدَّ الأَمَانَاتِ الَّتِي كَانَتْ مَعَ النَّبِيِّ ﷺ، إِلَى أَصْحَابِهاَ.

خَرَجَ النَّبِيُّ ﷺ، وَأَبُوبَكْرٍ إِلَى غَارِ ثَوْر وَمَكَثَ فِيهِ ثَلَاثَ لَيَالٍ. فِي هَذِهِ الأَيَام كَانَ عَبْدُ اللهِ بْنُ أَبِي بَكْرٍ يَذْهَبُ إِلَيْهِمَا بِأَخْبَارِ قُرَيْش، وَأُخْتُهُ أَسْمَاء تَأْتِيهِمَا بِالطَّعَامِ. وَاصَلَ ﷺ، وَأَبُوبَكْرٍ المَسِيرَ إِلَى المَدِينَةِ وَعِنْدَ وُصُولِهِمَا اِسْتَقْبَلَهُمَا أَهْلهَا بِالفَرَحِ وَالتَّكْبِير. نَزَلَ ﷺ، أَوَّلًا بِقُبَاء وَبَنَى بِهَا مَسْجِدَ قُبَاءٍ وَصَلَى بِهِ. بَعْدَ عِدَّةِ أَيَّامٍ دَخَلَ المَدِينَةَ وَبَنَى بِهَا المَسْجِدَ النَّبَوِيّ، وَآخَى بَيْنَ المُهَاجِرِينَ وَالأَنْصَارِ.

فِي المَدِينَةِ المُنَوَّرَةِ قَوِيَتْ شَوْكَةُ المُسْلِمِينَ وَبَدَأَتِ الدَّعْوَةُ فِي الاِنْتِشَارِ وَتَكَوَّنَتْ مَعَالِمُ الدَّوْلَةِ الإِسْلَامِيَّةِ هُنَاكَ، وَلِهَذا تُعْتَبَرُ الهِجْرَةُ إِلَى المَدِينَةِ حَدَثًا هَامًا فِي التَّارِيخِ الإِسْلَامِيِّ.

Migration to Medina

The infidels of Quraysh intensified their prosecution of Muslims and intended to assassinate the Prophet. The Prophet, peace be upon him, ordered his companions to migrate to Madinah after the people of Madinah pledged to give him shelter and protection. Muslims started to secretly migrate to Madinah for fear of the Quraysh. Umar ibn al-Khattab publicly emigrated.

The Prophet stayed in Makkah until Allah authorized him to emigrate. Then he told Abu Bakr to join him on his way to Madinah. He also asked Ali ibn Abi-Talib to sleep in his bed and wait in Makkah until all the properties that were kept with the Prophet be returned to their owners.

The Prophet and Abu Bakr went to the Thaur Cave and stayed there for three nights. While they were in the cave, Abu-Bakr's son, Abdullah, went to them with news of the nonbelievers, and his sister Asmaa brought them food. After three days, the Prophet and his friend, Abu Bakr, continued walking toward the city of Madinah. When they arrived, the people welcomed them with Takbeer, joy, and happiness.

The Prophet, peace be upon him, stayed in the city of Quba and built a Masjid in it, named Quba Masjid. After several days, he went to the City of Madinah and built his Masjid and established a brotherhood between the immigrants and the supporters. In Madinah, the Muslims became stronger and established the Islamic state. The immigration to Madinah is considered an essential event in the Islamic history.

غَزَوَاتُ الرَّسُولِ ﷺ
The Expeditions of the Prophet

بَدأَتْ غَزَوَاتُ الرَّسُولِ، ﷺ، فِي السَّنَةِ الثَّانِيَةِ لِلْهِجْرَةِ، بَعْدَ أنْ أَذِنَ اللهُ، عَزَّ وَجَلّ، لِلْمُسْلِمِينَ بِالقِتَالِ وَالدِّفَاعِ عَنْ أَنْفُسِهِم.

قَالَ اللهُ تَعَالَى: ﴿ أُذِنَ لِلَّذِينَ يُقَاتَلُونَ بِأَنَّهُمْ ظُلِمُوا وَإِنَّ اللهَ عَلَى نَصْرِهِمْ لَقَدِيرٌ﴾ [الحَجّ: 39-40].

وَفِي مَا يَلِي أَسْمَاءُ بَعْضِ الْغَزَوَاتِ:

1- غَزْوَةُ بَدْرٍ الكُبْرَى: وَقَعَتْ فِي السَّنَةِ الثَّانِيَةِ مِنَ الهِجْرَةِ، وَهِيَ أَوَّلُ مَعْرَكَةٍ مِنْ مَعَارِكِ الإِسْلَامِ. اِنْتَصَرَ فِيهَا المُسْلِمُونَ انْتِصَارًا كَبِيرًا، وَأَعَزَّ اللهُ بِهَا الإِسْلامَ وَالمُسْلِمِين.

2- غَزْوَةُ أُحُد: وَقَعَتْ فِي السَّنَةِ الثَّالِثَةِ مِنَ الهِجْرَةِ.

3- غَزْوَةُ الخَنْدَق (الأَحْزَاب):
وَقَعَتْ فِي السَّنَةِ الخَامِسَةِ مِنَ الهِجْرَةِ.

4- صُلْحُ الحُدَيْبِيَّة: وَقَعَ فِي السَّنَةِ السَّادِسَةِ مِنَ الهِجْرَةِ.

5- غَزْوَةُ خَيْبَر: وَقَعَتْ فِي السَّنَةِ السَّابِعَةِ مِنَ الهِجْرَةِ.

6- فَتْحُ مَكَّةَ: كَانَ فِي رَمَضَان فِي السَّنَةِ الثَّامِنَةِ مِنَ الهِجْرَةِ.

7- غَزْوَةُ حُنَيْن: وَقَعَتْ فِي السَّنَةِ الثَّامِنَةِ مِنَ الهِجْرَةِ.

8- غَزْوَةُ تَبُوك: وَقَعَتْ فِي السَّنَةِ التَّاسِعَةِ مِنَ الهِجْرَةِ، وَهِيَ آخِرُ مَغَازِيهِ ﷺ.

The Expeditions of the Prophet

In the second year of the Islamic Calendar, Allah permitted Muslims to fight their enemy and defend themselves.
Allah said: "Permission to fight is granted to those who have wronged, and Allah can give them (the believers) a victory." [22: 39-40].

Some of the Prophet's Expeditions are:

1. The Great Battle of Badr: It took place in the second year of migration and was the first battle of Islam. It was a significant event and ended with a great victory for Muslims.
2. The Battle of Uhud: It took place in the third year of migration.
3. The Battle of the Trench (Al-Ahzab): It took place in the fifth year of migration.
4. The Treaty of Hudaybiyah: It took place in the sixth year of migration.
5. The Battle of Khaibar: It took place in the seventh year of migration.
6. The Conquest of Makkah: It took place in the eighth year of migration.
7. The Battle of Hunayn: It took place in the eighth year of migration.
8. The Battle of Tabuk: It took place in the ninth year of migration, and it was the last Expedition of the Prophet.

غَزْوَةُ بَدْرٍ الكُبْرَى
The Great Battle of Badr

غَزْوَةُ بَدْرٍ، غَزْوَةٌ عَظِيمَةٌ - وَهِيَ أَوَّلُ مَعْرَكَةٍ مِنْ مَعَارِكِ الْإِسْلَامِ - وَقَعَتْ يَوْمَ الْجُمُعَةِ فِي السَّابعَ عَشَرَ مِنْ شَهْرِ رَمَضَانَ فِي السَّنَةِ الثَّانِيَةِ لِلْهِجْرَةِ. عَلِمَ النَّبِيُّ، ﷺ، بِقُدُومِ قَافِلَةٍ لِقُرَيْشٍ مِنَ الشَّامِ وَكَانَتْ مُكَوَّنَةٌ مِنْ أَلْفِ بَعِيرٍ بِقِيَادَةِ أَبِي سُفْيَانَ بْنِ حَرْب، فَاسْتَنْفَرَ الرَّسُولُ ﷺ، إِلَيْهَا أَصْحَابَهُ وَقَالَ: هَذِهِ عِيرُ قُرَيْشٍ فَاخْرُجُوا إِلَيْهَا لَعَلَّ اللهَ أَنْ يُنْفِلَكُمُوهَا وَذَلِكَ لاسْتِرْجَاعِ بَعْضِ الأَمْوَالِ الَّتِي قَامَتْ قُرَيْشُ بِالْاِسْتِيلَاءِ عَلَيْهَا عِنْدَمَا هَاجَرَ المُسْلِمُونَ مِنْ مَكَّةَ إِلَى الْمَدِينَةِ. خَرَجَ النَّبِيُّ ﷺ، وَمَعَهُ ثَلَاثِمِائَة وَثَلَاثَةَ عَشَرَ (وَقِيلَ ثَلَاثِمِائَة وَأَرْبَعَةَ عَشَرَ) رَجُلًا مِنَ الصَّحَابَةِ مَعَ فَرَسَيْنِ وَسَبْعُونَ بَعِيرًا حَتَّى نَزَلُوا بِبَدْرٍ. وَصَلَ الخَبَرُ إِلَى أَبِي سُفْيَان فَأَرْسَلَ إِلَى قُرَيْشٍ يُعْلِمُهُمْ بِذَلِكَ وَسَلَكَ بِالقَافِلَةِ طَرِيقًا غَيْرَ الطَّرِيقِ الرَّئِيسِيّ وَتَمَكَّنَ مِنَ الْفِرَارِ بِالْقَافِلَةِ. رَغْمَ نَجَاةِ الْقَافِلَةِ إِلَّا أَنَّ قُرَيْشًا أَصَرَّتْ عَلَى قِتَالِ الْمُسْلِمِين فَذَهَبَتْ إِلَى الْمَعْرَكَةِ بِأَلْفِ رَجُلٍ وَمِئَتَي فَرَس.

تَقَابَلَ الْجَيْشَانِ فِي بَدْرٍ وَعِنْدَمَا اِشْتَدَّ الْقِتَالُ دَعَا النَّبِيُّ، ﷺ، رَبَّهُ بِالنَّصْرِ، فَاسْتَجَابَ اللهُ لِدُعَائِهِ. اِنْتَهَتِ الْحَرْبُ بِانْتِصَارِ المُسْلِمِينَ عَلَى قُرَيْشٍ وَقُتِلَ فِي هَذِهِ المَعْرَكَةِ سَبْعُونَ مِنْ قُرَيْشٍ، وَتَمَّ أَسْرُ سَبْعُونَ آخَرُون وَاسْتُشْهِدَ مِنَ الْمُسْلِمِينَ أَرْبَعَةَ عَشَرَ صَحَابِيًّا.

غَزْوَةُ بَدْرٍ اِنْتَصَرَ فِيهَا المُسْلِمُونَ عَلَى قُرَيْشٍ، وَأَعَزَّ اللهُ بِهَا الإِسْلَامَ وَالمُسْلِمِينَ. قَالَ اللهُ تَعَالَى: ﴿وَلَقَدْ نَصَرَكُمُ اللهُ بِبَدْرٍ وَأَنْتُمْ أَذِلَّةٌ فَاتَّقُوا اللهَ لَعَلَّكُمْ تَشْكُرُونَ﴾ [آلِ عِمران: 123].

The Great Battle of Badr

The Great Battle of Badr was the first battle of Islam. It took place on Friday, the 17th of Ramadan, in the second year of migration. The Prophet, peace be upon him, learned that the Quraysh's caravan was coming from Shaam (Syria) and was made up of a thousand camels under the leadership of Abu Sufyan ibn Harb. The Prophet said to his companions: "This is the Quraysh's caravan. May Allah reward it to you as a replacement of the wealth the Quraysh took from you, go out and get it." The Prophet and three hundred thirteen (and some say three hundred fourteen) companions went to Badr to meet the caravan. Abu Sufyan received the news and he informed the Quraysh and changed the caravan route and escaped. The caravan arrived safely in Makkah, but the Quraysh insisted on fighting the Muslims. They went to battle with a thousand men and two hundred horses. The two armies met at Badr, and the Battle began. When the fighting intensified, the Prophet stood up, raised his hands, and asked Allah for victory, saying: "O Allah! Quraysh came with all their forces, challenging You and your Messenger. O Allah! Give us victory as You promised us." Allah answered his call. The Muslims fought bravely and won the battle. The battle resulted in seventy people killed and seventy captured from Quraysh, while only fourteen Muslims martyred." Allah mentioned the Battle of Badr in the Qur'an, by saying: "Allah gave you victory at Badr when you have been weak, so fear Allah, that you may be grateful." [3: 123].

Conquest of Makkah – فَتْحُ مَكَّةَ

نَقَضَتْ قُرَيْشٌ صُلْحَ الحُدَيْبِيَّةِ الَّذِي وَقَّعَتْهُ مَعَ النَّبِيِّ، ﷺ، فَأَمَرَ بِتَجْهِيزِ قُوَّةٍ عَسْكَرِيَّةٍ مِنْ عَشْرَةِ آلافِ مُقَاتِلٍ وَتَوَجَّهَ بِهِمْ إِلَى فَتْحِ مَكَّةَ. عِنْدَمَا وَصَلَ الجَيْشُ إِلَى مَكَّةَ، حَاصَرَهَا مِنْ أَرْبَعِ جِهَاتٍ وَكَانَ ذَلِكَ بِأَمْرٍ مِنَ الرَّسُولِ، ﷺ. هَذَا الحِصَارُ أَدْخَلَ الرُّعْبَ فِي قُلُوبِ أَهْلِ مَكَّةَ فَاسْتَسْلَمُوا، وَدَخَلَ النَّبِيُّ وَمَنْ مَعَهُ مَكَّةَ بِدُونِ قِتَالٍ. كَانَ فَتْحُ مَكَّةَ فِي شَهْرِ رَمَضَانَ فِي السَّنَةِ الثَّامِنَةِ مِنَ الهِجْرَةِ. عَامَلَ المُسْلِمُونَ أَهْلَ مَكَّةَ مُعَامَلَةً حَسَنَةً وَصَفَحَ النَّبِيُّ ﷺ، عَنْهُمْ، فَدَخَلَتِ القَبَائِلُ فِي دِينِ اللهِ أَفْوَاجًا، وَانْتَشَرَ الإِسْلَامُ فِي كُلِّ جَزِيرَةِ العَرَبِ، وَبِذَلِكَ كَانَ فَتْحُ مَكَّةَ فَتْحًا مُبَارَكًا لِلْمُسْلِمِينَ.

Quraysh broke the Hudiabyah treaty that was signed between them and the Prophet. So, the Prophet, peace be upon him, gathered an army of ten thousand men of his companions and headed to Makkah. When the Islamic army arrived in Makkah, the Prophet asked the army to siege the city from four sides. The siege made the people of Quraysh fearful and confused, so they surrendered. Muslims entered the city without a fight. The Prophet, peace be upon him, did not retaliate against the people of Makkah, but he treated them with respect and good manners. Also, he gave amnesty to everyone who no longer fought the Muslims. The excellent and proper treatment of the Prophet and his army has made Islam spread to all the Arabian Peninsula. The conquest of Makkah was a great victory for Muslims and one of the most significant events in Islamic History.

Death is a Reality - الْمَوْتُ حَقّ

قَالَ تَعَالَى: ﴿كُلُّ نَفْسٍ ذَائِقَةُ الْمَوْتِ﴾ [آلِ عِمران: 185].

وَقَالَ تَعَالَى: ﴿إِنَّكَ مَيِّتٌ وَإِنَّهُم مَّيِّتُونَ﴾ [الزُّمَر: 30] .

Allah said: "Every soul will taste death." [3: 185].
In another verse, Allah said: "Indeed, you "O (Muhammad) you will die, and verily they will die." [39: 30].

وَفَاةُ النَّبِيِّ ﷺ
The Death of the Prophet

بَعْدَ مُدَّةٍ قَصِيرَةٍ مِنْ حَجَّةِ الوَدَاعِ بَدَأَ الوَجَعُ يَظْهَرُ عَلَى رَسُولِ اللهِ ﷺ، ثمَّ اشْتَدَّ بِهِ الوَجَعُ فَاسْتَأْذَنَ أَزْوَاجَهُ فِي أنْ يَبْقَى فِي بَيْتِ عَائِشَةَ فَأَذِنَّ لَهُ، وَفَي ذَلِكَ كَانَتْ عَائِشَةُ، رَضِيَ اللهُ عَنْهَا، تَقُولُ: ((إِنَّ مِنْ نِعَمِ اللهِ عَلَيَّ أَنَّ رَسُولَ ﷺ، تُوُفِّيَ فِي بَيْتِي، وَفِي يَوْمِي، وَبَيْنَ سَحْرِي وَنَحْرِي)) [رَواه البُخارِي].

تُوُفِّيَ النَّبِيُّ ﷺ، يَوْمَ الإِثْنَيْنِ، الثَّانِيَ عَشَرَ مِنْ شَهْرِ رَبِيعِ الأَوَّلِ مِنَ السَّنَةِ الحَادِيَةَ عَشْرَةَ لِلْهِجْرَةِ، وَكَانَ لَهُ مِنَ العُمَرِ 63 عَامًا.

عَنْ هَذا الحَدَثِ الجَلَلِ قَالَ أَنَسُ بْنُ مَالِكٍ، رَضِيَ اللهُ عَنْهُ: ((لَمَّا كَانَ الْيَوْمُ الَّذِي دَخَلَ فِيهِ ﷺ، الْمَدِينَةَ أَضَاءَ مِنْهَا كُلُّ شَيْءٍ، فَلَمَّا كَانَ الْيَوْمُ الَّذِي مَاتَ فِيهِ أَظْلَمَ مِنْهَا كُلُّ شَيْءٍ، وَمَا نَفَضْنَا أَيْدِينَا مِنَ التُّرَابِ، وَإِنَّا لَفِي دَفْنِهِ ﷺ، حَتَّى أَنْكَرْنَا قُلُوبَنَا))
[جامع التِّرمذي]

The Death of the Prophet

After a short period, the Prophet, peace be upon him, departed Hajj, and the pain began to appear on him. When his pain intensified, he asked his wives for him to stay in the house of Aisha, and they all agreed. Aisha, may Allah be pleased with her, said: "One of the great favors of Allah on me, is that the Messenger of Allah, peace be upon him, died in my house, in my day, leaning on my chest." [Al-Bukhari].

The Prophet, peace be upon him, died on Monday 3/12/11 A.H. On this great tragedy, Anas ibn Malik, may Allah be pleased with him, said: "As for the day when the Messenger of Allah, peace be upon him, entered the city everything in it lit up. And on the day in which he died, everything in the city became dark. So, we shook our hands out of the dust, and we even denied our hearts." [At-Tirmidhi].

Children of the Prophet - أَبْنَاءُ النَّبِيِّ صلى الله عليه وسلم

رُزِقَ النَّبِيُّ ﷺ، بِسِتَّةِ أَبْنَاء مِنْ خَدِيجَةَ، رَضِيَ اللهُ عَنْهَا، وَهُمْ: القَاسِمُ، وَعَبْدُالله، وَزَيْنَبُ، وَرُقَيَّةُ، وَأُمُّ كَلْثُومٍ، وَفَاطِمَةُ.

وَرُزِقَ بِوَلَدِهِ إِبْرَاهِيمَ مِنْ مَارِيَةَ القُبْطِيَّةِ، رَضِيَ اللهُ عَنْهَا.

Allah Almighty gave the Prophet, Mohammad, peace be upon him, six children from Khadijah, may Allah be pleased with her. They are Al-Qasim, Abdullah, Zainab, Ruqaya, Umm Kulthum, and Fatima. Also, he had one son, Ibrahim, from Maria al-Qubtiya, may Allah be pleased with her.

حُقُوقُ النَّبِيِّ ﷺ، عَلَى أُمَّتِهِ
The Right of the Prophet on his Nation

حُقُوقُ النَّبِيِّ ﷺ، عَلَى أُمَّتِهِ كَثِيرَةٌ مِنْهَا:

♦- **الإيمَانُ بِأَنَّه رَسُولٌ مِنْ عِنْدِ اللهِ وَأَنَّهُ خَاتَمُ النَّبِيِّينَ، ﷺ**، قَالَ اللهُ تَعَالَى: ﴿مَّا كَانَ مُحَمَّدٌ أَبَا أَحَدٍ مِّن رِّجَالِكُمْ وَلَٰكِن رَّسُولَ اللهِ وَخَاتَمَ النَّبِيِّينَ﴾ [الأحْزاب: 40].

♦- **طَاعَتُهُ**، صلى الله عليه وسلم. قَالَ تَعَالَى: ﴿وَأَقِيمُوا الصَّلَاةَ وَآتُوا الزَّكَاةَ وَأَطِيعُوا الرَّسُولَ لَعَلَّكُمْ تُرْحَمُونَ﴾ [النُّور: 56].

♦- **اتِّبَاعُ سُنَّتِهِ**، ﷺ. قَالَ ﷺ: ((عَلَيْكُم بِسُنَّتِي وَسُنَّةِ الخُلَفَاءِ الرَّاشِدِين المَهْدِيِّينَ مِنْ بَعْدِي عَضُّوا عَلَيْهَا بِالنَّوَاجِذِ)). [أبو داودَ].

♦- **مَحَبَّتُهُ أكْثَر مِنَ النَّفْسِ**، قَالَ ﷺ: ((لَا يُؤْمِنُ أَحَدُكُمْ حَتَّى أَكُونَ أَحَبَّ إِلَيْهِ مِنْ وَالِدِهِ، وَوَلَدِهِ، وَالنَّاسِ أَجْمَعِينَ)) [البُخارِي وَمُسْلِم].

♦- **الصَّلَاةُ عَلَيْهِ** ﷺ، قَالَ تَعَالَى: ﴿إِنَّ اللهَ وَمَلَائِكَتَهُ يُصَلُّونَ عَلَى النَّبِيِّ يَا أَيُّهَا الَّذِينَ آمَنُوا صَلُّوا عَلَيْهِ وَسَلِّمُوا تَسْلِيمًا﴾[الأحْزاب: 56].

♦- **احْتِرَامُهُ، وتَوْقِيرُهُ، وَنُصْرَتُهُ** ﷺ، قَالَ اللهُ تَعَالَى: ﴿لِّتُؤْمِنُوا بِاللهِ وَرَسُولِهِ وَتُعَزِّرُوهُ وَتُوَقِّرُوهُ﴾ [الفَتح: 9]

♦- **عَدَمُ الْغُلُوِّ فِيهِ**، قَالَ ﷺ: ((لَا تُطْرُونِي، كَمَا أَطْرَتِ النَّصَارَى ابْنَ مَرْيَمَ، فَإِنَّمَا أَنَا عَبْدُهُ، فَقُولُوا عَبْدُ اللهِ، وَرَسُولُهُ)) [البُخارِي وَمُسْلِم].

The Rights of the Prophet ﷺ on his Nation

The Prophet, Muhammad, peace be upon him, has many rights on his Nation, including:

♦ - The belief that he is a messenger from Allah and the Seal of the Prophets. The Almighty Allah said: "Muhammad was not the father of any of your men, but he is the Messenger of Allah and the Seal of the Prophets." [33: 40].

♦ - Obey him and follow his Sunnah. Allah said: "Establish prayer and pay Zakah and obey the Messenger so that you may be merciful." [24: 56]. In another verse Allah said: "And follow him (Muhammad) that you may be guided." [7: 158].

♦ - Love him more than your soul. He, peace be upon him, said: "None of you will have true faith till he loves me more than his father, his children and all mankind." [Bukhari and Muslim].

♦ - Perform frequent prayer upon him. Allah said: "Surely Allah and His angels bless the Prophet [Muhammad], O you who believe send your prayers upon him and greet him, with a worthy greeting." [33: 56].

♦ - Respecting and honoring, peace be upon him. The Almighty Allah said: "To believe in Allah and His Messenger, you must help him and honor him and Glorify Allah in the morning and afternoon." [48: 9].

♦ - Do not exaggerate him. He, peace be upon him, said: "Do not exaggerate me as the Christians did to Jesus, son of Mary, but I am Allah's Slave and His Messenger." [Bukhari and Muslim].

أسْمَاءُ الْأنْبِيَاءِ وَالرُّسُلِ فِي الْقُرْآنِ الْكَرِيم

The Prophets and Messengers names in the Nobel Qur'an

مِنْ أَرْكَانِ الْإيمَانِ أَنْ يُؤْمِنَ الْمُسْلِمُ بِجَمِيعِ أَنْبِيَاءِ اللهِ وَرُسُلِهِ.
قَالَ تَعَالَى: ﴿آمَنَ الرَّسُولُ بِمَا أُنزِلَ إِلَيْهِ مِن رَّبِّهِ وَالْمُؤْمِنُونَ ۚ كُلٌّ آمَنَ بِاللهِ وَمَلَائِكَتِهِ وَكُتُبِهِ وَرُسُلِهِ لَا نُفَرِّقُ بَيْنَ أَحَدٍ مِّن رُّسُلِهِ﴾ [البقرة: 285].

وَيُؤْمِنُ المُسْلِمُ بِأَنَّ اللهَ تَعَالَى بَعَثَ فِي كُلِّ أُمَّةٍ رَسُولًا، مِنْهُمْ مَنْ ذَكَرَهُ لَنَا فِي كِتَابِهِ، الْقُرْآنِ الْكَرِيمِ، وَهَؤُلَاءِ يَجِبُ الْإيمَانُ بِهِمْ تَفْصِيلًا، وَمِنْهُمْ مَنْ لَمْ يُخْبِرْنَا عَنْهُمْ وَهَؤُلَاءِ يَجِبُ الْإيمَانُ بِهِمْ إِجْمَالًا. قَالَ تَعَالَى: ﴿وَلَقَدْ أَرْسَلْنَا رُسُلاً مِنْ قَبْلِكَ مِنْهُمْ مَنْ قَصَصْنَا عَلَيْكَ وَمِنْهُمْ مَنْ لَمْ نَقْصُصْ عَلَيْكَ﴾ [غافر: 78].

الْأَنْبِيَاءُ وَالرُّسُلُ الَّذِينَ ذَكَرَهُم اللهُ فِي الْقُرْآنِ الْكَرِيمِ خَمْسَةٌ وَعِشْرُونَ نَبِيًّا وَرَسُولًا، وَفِي مَا يَلِي قَائِمَة بِأَسْمَائِهِمْ، عَلَيْهِمُ السَّلَام.

One of the pillars of faith is that Muslims believe in all the Prophets and Messengers of Allah. The Almighty, Allah said: "The Messenger (Muhammad) believes in what has been revealed unto him from his Lord, and (so do) the believers. Each one believes in Allah, His Angels, His Books, and His Messengers." [2: 285]. Also, a Muslim believes that Allah has sent a Messenger to every nation. Some of the Prophets and Messengers have been mentioned by name in the Nobel Qur'an, but many have not been mentioned. Allah said: "And, indeed; We sent Messengers before you (O Muhammad), of some of them We have related to you their story and of some We have not related to you their story." [40: 78].

There are twenty-five Prophets and Messengers mentioned by Allah by name in the Holy Qur'an. The list of their names, peace be upon all of them, are:

أسْمَاءُ الْأنْبِيَاءِ وَالرُّسُلِ فِي الْقُرْآنِ الْكَرِيم **The Names of the Prophets and Messengers in the Nobel Qur'an**				
صَالِح Salih	هُود Hud	نُوح Noah	إدْرِيس Enoch	آدَم Adam
أيُّوب Job	إسْحَاق Isaac	إسْمَاعِيل Ishmael	إبْرَاهِيم Abraham	لُوط Lot
دَاوُد David	شُعَيْب Shu'aib	يُونُس Jonah	يُوسُف Joseph	يَعْقُوب Jacob
زَكَرِيَّا Zechariah	ذُو الْكِفْل Ezekiel	الْيَسَع Elisha	إلْيَاس Elias	سُلَيْمَان Solomon
مُحَمَّد صلى الله عليه وسلم Muhammad	عِيسَى Jesus	مُوسَى Moses	هَارُون Aaron	يَحْيَى John

أُمَّهَاتُ الْمُؤْمِنِين

Mothers of the Believers

قَالَ اللهُ تَعَالَى:

﴿النَّبِيُّ أَوْلَىٰ بِالْمُؤْمِنِينَ مِنْ أَنفُسِهِمْ وَأَزْوَاجُهُ أُمَّهَاتُهُمْ﴾

"The Prophet is closer to the Believers than their selves, and his wives are their mothers."

[33: 6][الأحزاب: 6]

أَسْمَاءُ أُمَّهَات الْمُؤْمِنِين Names of the mothers of Believers	
1- خَدِيجَةُ Khadija	6- أمّ سَلَمَة Umm-Salamah
2- سَوْدَةُ Souda	7- زَيْنَبُ بِنْتُ جَحْش Zainab bint Jahash
3- عَائِشَةُ Aisha	8- جُوَيْرِيَةُ Juwiariyah
4- حَفْصَةُ Hafsah	9- أُمُّ حَبِيبَة Umm-Habibah
5- زَيْنَبُ (أُمُّ المَسَاكِين) Zainab(Umm-Almaskeen	10- صَفِيَّةُ Safiyah
11- مَيْمُونَةُ Maimounah	

أُمَّهاتُ الْمُؤمِنِين رَضِيَ اللهُ عَنْهُنَّ
Mothers of the Believers

زَوْجَاتُ النَّبِيِّ ﷺ، أُمَّهَاتٌ لِلْمُؤْمِنِينَ، رَضِيَ اللهُ عَنْهُنَّ،
قَالَ اللهُ تَعَالَى: ﴿النَّبِيُّ أَوْلَىٰ بِالْمُؤْمِنِينَ مِنْ أَنفُسِهِمْ ۖ وَأَزْوَاجُهُ أُمَّهَاتُهُمْ﴾ [الأحزاب: 6].
وَقَدْ ذَكَرَ اللهُ تَعَالَى فِي القُرآنِ الكَرِيم أَنَّهُ ضَاعَفَ لَهُنَّ الأَجْرَ.
قَالَ تَعَالَى: ﴿وَمَن يَقْنُتْ مِنكُنَّ لِلَّهِ وَرَسُولِهِ وَتَعْمَلْ صَالِحًا نُّؤْتِهَا أَجْرَهَا مَرَّتَيْنِ﴾ [الأحزاب: 29].

The wives of the Prophet, peace be upon him, are the Mothers of the Believers. Allah, the Almighty, said: "The Prophet is closer to the Believers than their selves, and his wives are their mothers." [33: 6]. And Allah, the Almighty, has doubled their reward, He said: "If you (Wives of Prophet) desire Allah and His Messenger, and the hereafter, then verily, Allah shall double your reward!" [33: 29].

زَوْجَاتُ النَّبِيِّ صلى الله عليه وسلم
Wives of the Prophet

تَزَوَّجَ النَّبِيُّ، ﷺ، إِحْدَى عَشْرَةَ زَوْجَةً، هُنَّ أُمَّهَاتُ المُؤْمِنِينَ، وَفِي مَا يَلِي ذِكْرُ أَسْمَائِهِنَّ بِالتَّرْتِيبِ:

The Prophet, peace be upon him, married eleven wives. They are the mothers of the believers and their names are in order:

أَسْمَاءُ أمَّهَات الْمُؤمِنَين
Names of the Mothers of Believers

English	**Arabic**	**No.**
Khadija bint Khuwaylid (may Allah be pleased with her)	خَدِيجَةُ بِنْتُ خُوَيْلِدٍ رَضِيَ اللهُ عَنْهَا	1
Souda bint Zamua (may Allah be pleased with her)	سَوْدَةُ بِنْتُ زَمْعَةَ رَضِيَ اللهُ عَنْها	2
Aisha bint Abu Bakr Assidiq (may Allah be pleased with her)	عَائِشَةُ بِنْتُ أبِي بَكْرٍ الصِّدِّيق، رَضِيَ اللهُ عَنْهَا	3
Hafsah bint Umar ibn Al-Khattab (may Allah be pleased with her)	حَفْصَةُ بِنْتُ عُمَرَ بْنِ الخَطَّاب، رَضِيَ اللهُ عَنْهَا	4
Zainab bint Khuzaymah (may Allah be pleased with her)	زَيْنَبُ بِنْتُ خُزَيْمَةَ (أُمُّ المَسَاكِين) رَضِيَ اللهُ عَنْهَا	5
Umm-Salamah bint Abu Umayyah (may Allah be pleased with her)	أُمُّ سَلَمَةَ، هِنْدُ، بِنْتُ أبِي أُمَيَّة، رَضِيَ اللهُ عَنْهَا	6

Zainab bint Jahash (may Allah be pleased with her)	زَيْنَبُ بِنْتُ جَحْشٍ رَضِيَ اللهُ عَنْهَا	7
Juwiariyah bint al-Harith (may Allah be pleased with her)	جُوَيْرِيَةُ بِنْتُ الْحَارِثِ رَضِيَ اللهُ عَنْهَا	8
Umm-Habibah bint Abu Sufyan (may Allah be pleased with her)	أُمُّ حَبِيبَةَ، رَمْلَةُ، بِنْتُ أَبِي سُفْيَان، رَضِيَ اللهُ عَنْهَا	9
Safiya bint Huyay ibn Akhtab (may Allah be pleased with her)	صَفِيَّةُ بِنْتُ حُيَيِّ بِنْ أَخْطَب، رَضِيَ اللهُ عَنْهَا	10
Maimouna bint Al-Harith (may Allah be pleased with her)	مَيْمُونَةُ بِنْتُ الحَارِثِ الهِلَالِيَّة، رَضِيَ اللهُ عَنْهَا	11

عَلَى المُسْلِمِ مَعرِفَةُ أُمَّهَاتِ الْمُؤْمِنِينَ، وَالْإِعْتِرَافُ بِفَضْلِهِنَّ وَعُلُوِّ مَنْزِلَتِهِنَّ وَالتَّرَضِّي عَنْهُنَّ.

A Muslim has to know the mothers of the believers, recognize their high status and should say: "May Allah be pleased with them," when their names are mentioned.

الخُلَفَـاء الرَّاشِدُون
The Rightly Guided Caliphs

قَالَ رَسُولُ اللهِ ﷺ:

((عَلَيْكُمْ بِسُنَّتِي وَسُنَّةِ الْخُلَفَاءِ الرَّاشِدِينَ الْمَهْدِيِّينَ مِنْ بَعْدِي))

"Hold fast to my Sunnah and the Sunnah of the Rightly Guided Caliphs who will come after me."
[*Abu Dawud* and al-Tirmidhi]

أسْمَاء الخُلَفَاء الرَّاشِدِين بِالتَّرْتِيب The Rightly Guided Caliphs Names in Order	
1- أبُوبَكْرٍ الصِّدِّيق Abu Bakr As-Siddiq	3- عُثْمَانُ بْنُ عَفَّانَ Uthman ibn Affan
2- عُمَرُ بْنُ الخَطَّاب Umar ibn Al-Khattab	4- عَلِيٌّ بْنُ أَبِي طَالِبٍ Ali ibn Abi-Talib

الْخُلَفاءُ الرَّاشِدُون
The Rightly Guided Caliphs

الْخُلَفَاءُ الرَّاشِدُونَ هُمُ الصَّحَابَةُ الأَرْبَعَةُ الَّذِينَ تَوَلَّوْا الخِلَافَةَ بَعْدَ وَفَاةِ رَسُولِ اللهِ، ﷺ. الخُلَفَاءُ الرَّاشِدُونَ بِالتَّرْتِيبِ هُم: أبوبَكْرٍ الصِّدِّيقِ، وَعُمَرُ بْنُ الخطَّابِ، وَعُثمانُ بْنُ عفَّانَ، وَعَلِيُّ بْنُ أبِي طَالِبٍ، رَضِيَ اللهُ عَنْهُم جَمِيعًا. اِمْتازَ حُكْمُهُم بِالْعَدْلِ وَالأمْنِ وَالأمَانِ، وانتشر الإسلام فِي عَهْدِهِم شَرْقًا وغَرْبًا.

عَلَى الْمُسْلِمِ أنْ يُحِبَّهُمْ ويَتَرَضَّى عَنْهُمْ، وَأَنْ يَعْتَرِفَ بِفَضْلِهِمْ، وَيَدْرُسَ سِيرَتَهُمْ. اِعْلَمْ رَحِمَكَ اللهُ أَنَّ قَرْنَ الصَّحَابَةِ هُوَ خَيْرُ القُرُونِ، فَقَدْ صَحَّ عَنِ النَّبِيِّ ﷺ، أَنَّهُ قَالَ: ((خَيْرُ النَّاسِ قَرْنِي، ثُمَّ الَّذِينَ يَلُونَهُمْ، ثُمَّ الَّذِينَ يَلُونَهُمْ)) [البُخارِي ومُسْلِم].

The Rightly Guided Caliphs are the four companions who took over the affairs of Muslims after the death of Allah's Messenger, peace be upon him. They are Abu Bakr As-Siddiq, Umar ibn Al-Khattab, Uthman ibn Affan, and Ali ibn Abi-Talib, may Allah be pleased with them all. Their ruling is characterized by justice, security, and peace. During their time, Islam spread to the East and West.

A Muslim should love them, study their biography, admit their merit, and say: "May Allah be pleased with them," when their names are mentioned.

The Era of the companions is the best. The Prophet, peace be upon him, said: "The best of people are in my Era, then those that come after them, then those who come after them." [Al-Bukhari and Muslim].

Abu Bakr As-Siddiq – أَبُو بَكْرٍ الصِدّيق

1- أَبُو بَكْرٍ الصِدّيق، رَضِيَ اللهُ عَنْهُ، اِسْمُهُ عَبْدُ اللهِ بْنُ أَبِي قُحَافَةَ، التَّيْمِيّ القُرَشِيّ، وُلِدَ بِمَكَّةَ.

2- هُوَ أَوَّلُ الخُلَفَاءِ الرَّاشِدِينَ، وَأَوَّلُ مَنْ أَسْلَمَ مِنَ الرِّجَالِ، وَأَحَدُ العَشَرَةِ المُبَشّرِينَ بِالجَنَّةِ.

3- أَسْلَمَ عَلَى يَدَيْهِ عَدَدٌ مِنْ كِبَارِ الصَّحَابَةِ، مِنْهُمْ: عُثْمَانُ بْنُ عَفَّانَ، وَسَعْدُ بْنُ أَبِي وَقَّاصٍ، وَعَبْدُالرَحْمَن بْنُ عَوْفٍ.

4- كَانَ رَضِيَ اللهُ عَنْهُ، مِنْ أَحَبِّ الصَّحَابَةِ لِرَسُولِ اللهِ ﷺ، وَكَانَ رَفِيقُهُ فِي الهِجْرَةِ مِنْ مَكَّةَ إِلَى المَدِينَةِ.

5- شَهِدَ بَدْرًا وَكُلّ الغَزَوَاتِ مَعَ رَسُولِ اللهِ ﷺ، وَأَنْفَقَ كُلَّ مَالِه فِي سَبِيلِ اللهِ.

6- اِشْتَهَرَ أَبُوبَكْرٍ بِمَعْرِفَةِ عِلْمِ الأَنْسَابِ وَأَخْبَارِ العَرَب.

مِنْ أَهَمّ أعْمَالِه:

1- مُحَارَبَةُ المُرْتَدّينَ وَمَانِعِي الزَّكَاةِ. اِرْتَدَّتْ بَعْضُ القَبَائِلِ عَنِ الْإِسْلَامِ وَامْتَنَعَتْ عَنْ أَدَاءِ الزَّكَاةِ، فَقَرَّرَ، رَضِيَ اللهُ عَنْهُ، بِحَزْمٍ وَقُوَّةٍ قِتَالَهُم وَالقَضَاءَ عَلَيْهِم.

2- إِنْفَاذُ جَيْشِ أُسَامَةَ لِمُحَارَبَةِ الرُّوم.

3- فِي عَهْدِهِ تَمَّ فَتْح جُزْءًا مِنَ العِرَاقِ وَالشَّامِ.

4- أَمَرَ بِجَمْعِ الْقُرْآنِ الْكَرِيمِ بِمَشُورَةٍ مِنْ عُمَرَ، وَكَلَّفَ بِذَلِكَ المَهَمَّةِ زَيْدَ بْنَ ثَابِتٍ، رَضِيَ اللهُ عَنْهُ.

اِسْتَمَرَّتْ خِلَافَتهُ مَا يُقَارِبُ السَّنَتَيْنِ. تُوُفِّيَ رَضِيَ اللهُ عَنْهُ، سَنَةَ 13 هـ، وَدُفِنَ فِي حُجْرَةِ اِبْنَتِهِ، عَائِشَةَ، بِجِوَارِ رَسُولِ اللهِ، ﷺ.

Abu Bakr As-Siddiq

1. Abu Bakr As-Siddiq, may Allah be pleased with him, was named Abdullah ibn Abi Quhafa, al-Taymi, al-Qurashi, and he was born in Makkah.

2. He was the first of the Rightly Guided Caliphs, the first man to embrace Islam, and one of the ten companions, who was given the glad tidings of paradise.

3. Because of his effort, several senior companions embraced Islam, including: (Uthman ibn Affan, Saad ibn Abi Waqas, and Abdul-Rahman ibn Auf).

4. He was a close friend to the Messenger of Allah and was his companion in the migration to Madinah.

5. He took part in all battles with the Messenger of Allah, and he spent all his money for the sake of Allah.

6. He was famous for his knowledge of genealogy and Arab news.

Among his most famous works:

1. When some tribes refrained from Islam and abstained from paying Zakah, Abu Bakr decided firmly and forcefully to fight them, and he was victorious.

2. He sent the army of Osama to fight the Romans.

3. During his reign, Iraq and Syria were conquered.

4. He ordered to collect the writings of Qur'an on the advice of Umar. His succession lasted nearly two years. He died in the year 13 AH, and was buried in the room of his daughter Aisha, next to the Messenger of Allah, peace be upon him.

Umar ibn Al-Khattab – عُمَرُ بْنُ الخَطَّاب

1- عُمَرُ بْنُ الخَطَّابِ، رَضِيَ اللهُ عَنْهُ، هُوَ أمِيرُ المُؤْمِنِينَ، العَدَوِيُّ القُرَشِيُّ، وُلِدَ بِمَكَّةَ.

2- هُوَ ثَانِيَ الخُلَفَاءِ الرَّاشِدِينَ، وَأحَدُ العَشَرَةِ المُبَشّرِينَ بِالجَنَّةِ.

3- شَهِدَ بَدْرًا وَكُلَّ الغَزَوَاتِ مَعَ رَسُولِ اللهِ ﷺ، وَكَانَ شُجَاعًا تَحَدَّى قُرَيْشًا وَهَاجَرَ إلَى المَدِينَةِ فِي وَضَحِ النَّهَارِ.

4- اِشْتَهَرَ عُمَرُ بِالْعَدْلِ وَالإنْصَافِ وَالقُوَّةِ فِي الحَقِّ، قَالَ لَهُ النَّبِيُّ، ﷺ: ((وَالَّذِي نَفْسِي بِيَدِهِ مَا لَقِيَكَ الشَّيْطَانُ قَطُّ سَالِكًا فَجًّا إلاَّ سَلَكَ فَجًّا غَيْرَ فَجِّكَ)) [رَوَاهُ البُخَارِي وَمُسْلِمٌ].

5- كَانَ عُمَرُ مِنْ كِبَارِ الصَّحَابَةِ، وَكَانَ مُتَوَاضِعًا فِي حَيَاتِهِ وَفِي مُعَامَلَتِهِ لِلنَّاسِ مَعَ الحَزْمِ فِي الدِّين.

مِنْ أهَمِّ أعْمَالِهِ:

1- اِنْتَشَرَ الإسْلَامُ فِي عَهْدِهِ وَوَصَلَتِ الفُتُوحَاتُ الإسْلَامِيَّةُ إلَى الشَّامِ، وَمِصْرَ، وَشَمَالِ أفْرِيقِيا، وَبِلَادِ فَارِس.

2- أسَّسَ نِظَامَ الدَّوَاوِين مِثْلَ دِيوَانِ الجِبَايَةِ وَدِيوَانِ العَطَاءِ وَقَامَ بِتَأسِيس بَيْتِ مَالِ المُسْلِمِين.

3- نَظَّمَ الجَيْشَ وَالشُّرْطَةَ وَأقَامَ المَحَاكِمَ وَعَيَّنَ لَهَا القُضَاةَ.

4- أنْشَأَ التَّقْوِيمَ الهِجْرِيّ، وَقَامَ بِإنْشَاءِ مَدِينَةِ الكُوفَة وَالفُسْطَاط وَمَهَّدَ الطُّرُقَ.

اِسْتَمَرَّتْ مُدَّةُ خِلَافَتِهِ عَشْرَ سَنَوَاتٍ وَسِتَّة أشْهُرٍ. تُوُفِّيَ رَضِيَ اللهُ عَنْه، سَنَة 23 هـ، وَدُفِنَ بِجِوَارِ النَّبِيِّ، ﷺ، وَأبُو بَكْرٍ الصَّدِيقِ، رَضِيَ اللهُ عَنْهُ.

Umar ibn Al-Khattab

1. Umar ibn al-Khattab, Adawi al-Qureshi, may Allah be pleased with him, was born in Makkah.

2. He was the second of the Rightly Guided Caliphs and one of the ten companions who was given the glad tidings of paradise.

3. He was brave and took part in all the battles with the Messenger of Allah, peace be upon him.

4. Umar is known for his justice and authority. Allah's Messenger, peace be upon him, said to him: "By Him in Whose Hands my life is, whenever Satan sees you taking a path, he will take a path other than yours." [Al-Bukhari and Muslim].

5. He was a senior companion, modest in his life and his treatment of people with ffirmness in religion.

Among his most famous works:

1. During his reign, the Islamic State expanded and reached Syria, Egypt, North Africa, and Persia.

2. He established many institutions in the state; One of which was the house of the Muslim treasury.

3. He organized the army, the police departments, and appointed judges to the courts.

4. He established and enforced the Hijri calendar, built new cities, including Kufa and Fustat, and paved the roads.

His succession lasted ten years and six months and he, may Allah be pleased with him, died in the year 23 AH, and was buried alongside the Prophet, peace be upon him, and Abu Bakr, may Allah be pleased with him.

Uthmanibn Affan – عُثْمَانُ بْنُ عَفَّانَ

1- عُثْمَانُ بْنُ عَفَّانَ الْأَمَوِيُّ الْقُرَشِيُّ، رَضِيَ اللهُ عَنْهُ، وُلِدَ بِمَكَّةَ سَنَةَ 47 قَبْلَ الْهِجْرَةِ، وَكَانَ مِنَ السَّابِقِينَ إِلَى الْإِسْلَامِ.

2- هُوَ ثَالِثُ الْخُلَفَاءِ الرَّاشِدِينَ، وَأَحَدُ الْعَشَرَةِ الْمُبَشَّرِينَ بِالْجَنَّةِ.

3- تَزَوَّجَ اِثْنَتَيْنِ مِنْ بَنَاتِ النَّبِيِّ صلى الله عليه وسلم - تَزَوَّجَ رُقَيَّةَ وَبَعْدَ وَفَاتِهَا تَزَوَّجَ أُخْتَهَا، أُمَّ كَلْثُومٍ- وَكَانَ مِنْ أَوَائِلِ مَنْ هَاجَرَ إِلَى أَرْضِ الْحَبَشَةِ.

4- بُويِعَ عُثْمَانُ بِالْخَلَافَةِ بَعْدَ وَفَاةِ عُمَرَ بْنِ الْخَطَّابِ.

5- اِشْتَهَرَ رَضِيَ اللهُ عَنْهُ، بِالْإِنْفَاقِ فِي سَبِيلِ اللهِ، وَبِالْحَيَاءِ، قَالَ عَنْهُ رَسُولُ اللهِ صلى الله عليه وسلم: ((أَشَدُّ أُمَّتِي حَيَاءً عُثْمَانُ بْنُ عَفَّانَ)) [صحيح الجامع لِلألباني].

6- جَهَّزَ جَيْشَ الْعُسْرَةِ الَّذِي تَوَجَّهَ لِلِقَاءِ الرُّومِ، فَقَالَ صلى الله عليه وسلم: ((مَا ضَرَّ عُثْمَانَ مَا عَمِلَ بَعْدَ الْيَوْمِ)) [صحيح التّرمذي].

مِنْ أَهَمِّ أَعْمَالِهِ:

1- جَمَعَ الْقُرْآنَ الْكَرِيمَ فِي مُصْحَفٍ وَاحِدٍ، ثُمَّ بَعَثَ بِنُسَخٍ مِنْهُ إِلَى الْأَمْصَارِ.

2- أَنْشَأَ أَوَّلَ أُسْطُولٍ بَحْرِيٍّ إِسْلَامِيٍّ.

3- تَمَّ فِي عَهْدِهِ فَتْحُ أَرْمِينِيَةَ وَطَرَابُلُسَ الشَّامِ وَجَزِيرَةَ قُبْرُصٍ.

اِسْتَمَرَّتْ خِلَافَتُهُ، رَضِيَ اللهُ عَنْهُ، مَا يُقَارِبُ اِثْنَي عَشَرَ عَامًا. تُوُفِّيَ رَضِيَ اللهُ عَنْهُ، بِالْمَدِينَةِ سَنَةَ 35 هـ وَدُفِنَ بِالْبَقِيعِ.

Uthman ibn Affan

1. Uthman ibn Affan al-Umawi al-Qurashi, may Allah be pleased with him, was born in Makkah, and was one of the earliest to embrace Islam.

2. He was the third of the Rightly Guided Caliphs and one of the ten companions, who was given the glad tidings of paradise.

3. His nickname is "Zu-Noorain" because he married two daughters of the Prophet (Rukaiya and after her death he married Umm Kulthum).

4. He was the first companion to immigrate to Abyssinia.

5. He was well-known for spending generously for the sake of Allah, and also for his modesty. The Prophet, peace be upon him, said: "The most modest man from my Ummah (nation) is Uthman ibn Affan." [Al Albani, in Saheeh Al Jama'a].

6. He equipped the army that went to Tabuk to meet with the Romans, so the Prophet said about him: "Nothing will harm Uthman after this day, whatever he does." [Albani, in Saheeh At-Tirmidhi].

Among his most famous works:

1. He ordered to compile the Nobel Qur'an into a single book (called Al-Mushaf). He kept one copy for himself and sent copies to all the Islamic cities.

2. He established the first Islamic fleet.

3. During his reign, Armenia, Tripoli of Sham, and the Island of Cyprus were conquered.

His succession lasted nearly 12 years, and he died in the year 35 AH in Madinah.

Ali ibn Abi-Taleb – عَلِيُّ بْنُ أبي طَالِب

1- عَلِيُّ بْنُ أَبِي طَالِب الهَاشِمِيّ القُرَشِيّ، رَضِيَ اللهُ عَنْهُ، وُلِدَ بِمَكَّةَ قَبْلَ البِعْثَةِ بِعَشْرِ سِنِين.

2- هُوَ رَابِعُ الخُلَفَاءِ الرَّاشِدِينَ، وَأَحَدُ العَشَرَةِ المُبَشّرِينَ بِالجَنَّةِ.

3- تَرَبَّى عَلِيٌّ فِي بَيْتِ النُّبُوَّة، وَكَان أَوَّلَ مَنْ أَسْلَمَ مِنَ الصِّبْيَانِ وَهُوَ اِبْنُ عَمِّ النَّبِيِّ وَصِهْرُهُ – زَوْجُ فَاطِمَةَ، رَضِيَ اللهُ عَنْهَا.

4- اِشْتَهَرَ عَلِيٌّ بِالْفَصَاحَةِ وَالشَّجَاعَةِ وَالْعَدْلِ، وَشَهِدَ كُلَّ المَشَاهِدِ مَعَ النَّبِي، صلى الله عليه وسلم، إلّا غَزْوَةَ تَبُوك، لِأنَّ النَّبِيَّ صلى الله عليه وسلم، اِسْتَخْلَفَهُ عَلَى المَدِينَةِ، وَقَالَ لَهُ: ((أَمَا تَرْضَى أَنْ تَكُونَ مِنِّي بِمَنْزِلَةِ هَارُونَ مِنْ مُوسَى إِلَّا أَنَّهُ لَا نَبِيَّ بَعْدِي)) [البُخارِي ومُسْلِم].

مِنْ أَهَمِّ أعْمَالِهِ:

1- نَظَّمَ الْأَسْوَاقَ وَحَثَّ عَلَى التَّعَامُلِ بِالشَّرْعِ فِي التِّجَارَةِ.

2- نَظَّمَ جِهَازَ الشُّرْطَةِ وَالقَضَاء.

3- حَارَبَ الخَوَارِجَ وَاستَطَاعَ القَضَاءَ عَلَيْهِمْ.

اِسْتَمَرَّتْ خِلَافَتُهُ خَمْسَ سَنَوَاتٍ وَثَلَاثَةَ أَشْهُرٍ. تُوُفِيَّ رَضِيَ اللهُ عَنْهُ، فِي رَمَضَانَ سَنَةَ 40 هـ، وَدُفِنَ بِالكُوفَة.

Ali ibn Abi-Talib

1. Ali ibn Abi Talib Al-Hashimi Al-Qurashi, may Allah be pleased with him, was born in Makkah, ten years before the migration to Madinah.

2. He is the fourth of the Rightly Guided Caliphs and one of the ten given glad tidings of Paradise.

3. He was raised in the house of prophecy, and was the first to become Muslim of the two boys, the cousin and son-in-law of the Prophet - the husband of Fatima, may Allah be pleased with her.

4. He was famous for his audacity, courage, and justice. He took part in all battles with the Messenger of Allah, peace be upon him, except the Battle of Tabuk. The Prophet went to the Battle of Tabuk and appointed Ali as a governor on Madinah, and said to him: "Will you not be satisfied, that you are to me of the status of Harun (Aron) to Musa (Moses), except that, there is no prophet after me." [Al-Bukhari and Muslim].

Among his most famous works:

1- He organized the market systems and urged people to deal with Sharia in trade.

2- He regulated the police and judiciary systems.

3- He fought the Khawarij and defeated them.

His succession lasted five years and three months. He died in Ramadan in the year 40 AH, in the city of Kufah.

العَشْرَةُ المُبَشّرُونَ بِالجَنَّةِ

The Ten with Glad Tidings of Paradise

1- أبُوبَكْرٍ الصِّدّيق Abu Bakr As-Siddiq	6- الزُّبَيْرُ بْنُ العَوَّام Zubayr ibn Al-Awam
2- عُمَرُ بْنُ الخطَاب Umar ibn Al-Khattab	7- عَبدُ الرَّحْمَنِ بْنِ عَوْف Abdul-Rahman ibn Auf
3- عُثْمَانُ بْنُ عَفَّان Uthman ibn Affan	8- سَعْدُ بْنُ أبِي وَقَّاص Sa'ad ibn Abi-Waqqas
4- عَلِيُّ بْنُ أبِي طَالِب Ali ibn Abi-Talib	9- سَعِيدُ بْنُ زَيْد Sa'eed ibn Zaid
5- طَلْحَةُ بْنُ عُبَيْدِ الله Talha ibn Ubaidu-Allah	10- أبُوعُبَيْدَةَ عَامِرُ بْنُ الجَرَّاح Abu Abeida Amer ibn Jarrah

العَشْرَةُ المُبَشّرُونَ بِالجَنَّةِ
The Ten with Glad Tidings of Paradise

الصَّحَابَةُ رَضِيَ اللهُ عَنْهُمْ جَمِيعًا، آمَنُوا بِاللهِ وَرَسُولِهِ وَبَذَلُوا فِي سَبِيلِ اللهِ الْأَنْفُسَ وَالْأَهْلَ، وَالْأَمْوَالَ وَالدِّيَارَ.

الصَّحَابَةُ أَثْنَى عَلَيْهِم اللهُ- عَزَّ وَجَلَّ- فِي كِتَابِهِ العَزِيز. قَالَ تَعَالَى: ﴿وَالسَّابِقُونَ الْأَوَّلُونَ مِنَ الْمُهَاجِرِينَ وَالْأَنصَارِ وَالَّذِينَ اتَّبَعُوهُم بِإِحْسَانٍ رَّضِيَ اللهُ عَنْهُمْ وَرَضُوا عَنْهُ﴾ [التَّوْبة: 100].

وَأَثْنَى عَلَيْهِم رَسُولُ اللهِ ﷺ، بِقَوْلِهِ: ((خَيرُ النَّاسِ قَرْنِي ، ثُمَّ الَّذِينَ يَلُونَهُم ، ثُمَّ الَّذِينَ يَلُونَهُم)) [البُخارِي وَمُسْلِم].

بَشَّرَ رَسُولُ اللهِ ﷺ، عَدَدًا مِنْ أَصْحَابِهِ بِالجَنّةِ (مِنَ الرِّجَالِ وَالنِّسِاء)، ولَكِن جَاءَ ذكر عشرة مِنْهُم فِي حَدِيثٍ وَاحِدٍ فَاشْتَهَرُوا – بِالْعَشْرَةِ المُبَشّرِينَ بِالجَنَّةِ.

قَالَ رَسُولُ اللهِ ﷺ: ((أَبُو بَكْرٍ فِي الْجَنَّةِ، وَعُمَرُ فِي الْجَنَّةِ، وَعُثْمَانُ فِي الْجَنَّةِ، وَعَلِيٌّ فِي الْجَنَّةِ، وَطَلْحَةُ فِي الْجَنَّةِ، وَالزُّبَيْرُ فِي الْجَنَّةِ، عَبدُ الرَّحْمَـٰنِ بْن عَوْفٍ فِي الْجَنَّةِ، وَسَعْدٌ [بِن أَبِي وَقَّاصٍ] فِي الْجَنَّةِ، وَسَعِيدٌ [بِن زَيْدٍ] فِي الْجَنَّةِ، وَأَبُو عُبَيْدَةَ بْنُ الْجَرَّاحِ فِي الْجَنَّةِ)) [أبو داود والتّرمذي وأحمد].

The companions, may Allah be pleased with them, believed in Allah and His Messenger. They sacrificed their lives, wealth, families, and homes for the sake of Allah. Because of their effort, Allah praised them by saying: "And the first people to become Muslim from the immigrants and supporters and those who followed them on the right path, Allah is pleased with them and they are pleased with Him." [9: 100].

The Messenger of Allah, peace be upon him, praised them by saying: "The best people are the people of my generation, then those who follow them, and then those who follow them." [Al-Bukhari, Muslim].

The companions are the best people in the Ummah (nation) of Islam. Every Muslim should love them and ask Allah to be pleased with them. The Prophet, peace be upon him, gave glad tidings of paradise to several companions. Ten of their names are mentioned in one Hadith, so they became known as "The Ten with Glad Tidings of Paradise." The Prophet, peace be upon him, said: "Abu Bakr is in Paradise, Umar is in Paradise, Uthman is in Paradise, Ali is in Paradise, Talan is in Paradise, Az-Zubair is in Paradise, Abdu Rahman ibn Away is in Paradise, Said [ibn Abi Waqqas] is in Paradise, Sa'eed [ibn Zayd] is in Paradise, and Abu Ubaidah ibn Al-Jarrah is in Paradise." [at-Tirmidhi and Ahmed].

Note - مُلَاحَظَة

هَذَا الحَدِيثُ يُوَضِّحُ أَنَّ الخُلَفَاءَ الرَّاشِدِينَ الأَرْبَعَة: أَبَابَكْرٍ، وَعُمَرَ، وَعُثْمَانَ، وَعَلِيَّ، رَضِيَ اللهُ عَنْهُم، هُمْ مِنْ أَوَائِلِ الْعَشَرَةِ الْمُبَشَّرِينَ بِالْجَنَّةِ وَقَدْ تَكَلَّمْنَا عَنْهِمْ فِي الْفَصْلِ السَّابِقِ وَالآنَ نَتَكَلَّمُ عَنِ السِّتَّةِ الْبَاقِين:

This Hadith shows the four guided Caliphs (Abu Bakr, Umar, Uthman, and Ali) were among the ten companions who were given the glad tidings of Paradise.
Now we will talk about the other six companions.

Talha ibn Ubaidu-Allah – طَلْحَةُ بْنُ عُبَيْدِ الله

هُوَ أَحَدُ الْأَوائِلِ السَّابِقِينَ إِلَى الإِسْلامِ، شَارَكَ فِي جَمِيعِ الْغَزَواتِ إِلَّا غَزْوَةَ بَدْرٍ لِأَنَّهُ كَانَ وَقْتَهَا بِالشَّامِ. قَالَ عَنْهُ النَّبِيُّ صلى الله عليه وسلم: ((مَنْ سَرَّهُ أَنْ يَنْظُرَ إِلَى شَهِيدٍ يَمْشِي عَلَى وَجْهِ الأَرْضِ فَلْيَنْظُرْ إِلَى طَلْحَةَ بْنِ عُبَيْدِ اللَّهِ)) [رواه الترمذي وصححه الألباني].

كَانَ طَلْحَةُ أَحَدَ السِّتَّةِ الَّذِينَ اِخْتَارَهُمْ عُمَرُ بْنُ الخَطَّاب لِيَخْتَارُوا الْخَلِيفَةَ مِنْ بَعْدِهِ، تُوُفِّيَ رَضِيَ اللهُ عَنْهُ، سَنَةَ 36 هـ.

Talha ibn Ubaidu-Allah was one of the first few to embrace Islam. He took part in all invasions with the Prophet, peace be upon him, but he did not join the Battle of Badr because he was on duty in Sham. The Prophet, peace be upon him, said: “Whoever would like to see a martyr walking on the face of the earth, have him look at Talhah ibn Ubaidu-Allah.”

He was one of the six members, who were chosen by Umar to choose the Caliph after him. He died in the year 36 AH.

Zubayr ibn Al-Awam – الزُّبَيْرُ بْنُ العَوَّامِ

هُوَ أَحَدُ الْأَوائِلِ السَّابِقِينَ إِلَى الإِسْلَامِ، وَهُوَ اِبْنُ عَمَّةِ النَّبِيِّ صلى الله عليه وسلم . يُلَقَّبُ الزُّبَيْرُ بِحَوارِيِّ رَسُولِ اللهِ، وَكَانَ أَوَّلُ مَنْ سَلَّ سَيْفَهُ فِي الإِسْلَامِ وشَارَكَ فِي جَمِيعِ الغَزَواتِ مَعَ النَّبِيِّ، صلى الله عليه وسلم. كَانَ الزُّبَيْرُ أَحَدَ السِّتَّةِ الَّذِينَ اِخْتَارَهُمْ عُمَرُ بْنُ الخَطَّابِ لِيَخْتَارُوا الْخَلِيفَةَ مِنْ بَعْدِهِ وَشَارَكَ فِي فَتْحِ مِصْرَ. تُوُفِّيَ رَضِيَ اللهُ عَنْهُ، سَنَةَ 32 هـ.

Zubayr ibn Al-Awam was one of the first few to embrace Islam and was a cousin of the Prophet, peace be upon him.

Zubayr was known as a disciple of the Prophet and was the first man to use his sword in Islam. He participated in all battles with the Prophet, and was one of the six members, who were chosen by Umar to choose the Caliph after him.
Also, he participated in the conquest of Egypt and died in the year 36 AH.

Abdul-Rahman ibn Auf – عَبدُ الرَّحْمَـٰنِ بْنُ عَوْفٍ

هُوَ أَحَدُ الأَوائِلِ السَّابِقِينَ إِلَى الإِسْلَامِ. شَارَكَ فِي جَمِيعِ الغَزَوَاتِ مَعَ النَّبِيِّ ﷺ. كَانَ عَبدُ الرَّحْمَـٰنِ تَاجِرًا ثَرِيًّا وَكَرِيمًا، تَصَدَّقَ مَرَّةً بِنِصْفِ مَالِهِ، وَكَانَ يَتَصَدَّقُ بِسَخَاءٍ كُلَّمَا احْتَاجَ المُسْلِمُونَ لِذَلِكَ. هَاجَرَ إِلَى الحَبَشَةِ ثُمَّ إِلَى المَدِينَةِ وَشَارَكَ فِي جَمِيعِ الغَزَوَاتِ مَعَ النَّبِيِّ ﷺ.

كَانَ عَبدُ الرَّحْمَـٰنِ أَحَدَ السِّتَّةِ الَّذِينَ اِخْتَارَهُمْ عُمَرُ بْنُ الخَطَّابِ لِيَخْتَارُوا الْخَلِيفَةَ مِنْ بَعْدِهِ. تُوُفِّيَ رَضِيَ اللهُ عَنْهُ، بِالمَدِينَةِ وَصَلَّى عَلَيْهِ عُثْمَانُ بْنُ عَفَّانَ وَدُفِنَ بِالبَقِيعِ سَنَةَ 32 هـ.

Abdul Rahman ibn Auf was one of the first few to embrace Islam. He participated in all the invasions during the Prophet's era. He was a wealthy merchant and was well-known for spending generously for the sake of Allah. He once donated half his wealth and was generous in charity whenever Muslims were in need. He was one of the six men, who were chosen by Umar to select the successor after him.
He immigrated to Abyssinia and then to Madinah. He participated in all battles with the Prophet, peace be upon him. He died in Madinah in the year 32 AH.

Sa’ad ibn Abi-Waqqas – سَعْدُ بْنُ أَبِي وَقَّاصٍ

هُوَ أَحَدُ الأَوَائِلِ السَّابِقِينَ إِلَى الإِسْلَامِ، وَهُوَ أَوَّلُ مِنْ رَمَى بِسَهْمٍ فِي سَبِيلِ اللهِ، قَالَ لَهُ النَّبِيّ ﷺ، فِي أَحَدِ الغَزَوَاتِ: ((ارْمِ سَعْدُ فِدَاكَ أَبِي وَأُمِّي))، وَقَدْ شَهِدَ الْمَشَاهِدَ كُلَّهَا مَعَ النَّبِيِّ ﷺ. شَارَكَ فِي مَعْرَكَةِ الْقَادِسِيَّة، وَتَوَلَّى قِيَادَةَ الجَيْشِ الَّذِي فَتَحَ مَدَائِنَ كِسْرَي بِالعِرَاقِ وَبِلَادَ فَارِسٍ.

كَانَ سَعْدُ أَحَدَ السِّتَّةِ الَّذِينَ اِخْتَارَهُمْ عُمَرُ بْنُ الخَطَّاب لِيَخْتَارُوا الْخَلِيفَةَ مِنْ بَعْدِهِ، وَكَانَ أَحَدُ الَّذِينَ اِعْتَزَلُوا الفِتْنَةَ الَّتِي حَدَثَتْ بَيْنَ الصَّحَابَةِ. تُوُفِّيَ رَضِيَ اللهُ عَنْهُ، سَنَةَ 55 هـ وَدُفِنَ بَالمَدِينَةِ.

Sa’ad ibn Abi-Waqqas was one of the first few to embrace Islam. He was the first Muslim to throw an arrow for the sake of Allah. In one of the battles, the Prophet said to him: “Shoot Sa’ad Fedak, my father, and my mother.” He participated in all battles with the Prophet, and he led the army in the battle of Qadisiya, which opened part of Iraq and Persia. Sa’ad was one of the six men, who were chosen by Umar to select the successor after him. Also, he was one of those who quit the trial that occurred between the companions. He died, may Allah be pleased with him, in the year 55 AH and was buried in the city of Madinah.

Sa’eed ibn Zaid – سَعِيدُ بْنُ زَيْد

هُوَ أَحَدُ الأَوَائِلِ السَّابِقِينَ إِلَى الإِسْلَامِ، حَيْثُ أَسْلَمَ وَأَسْلَمَتْ مَعَهُ زَوْجَتُهُ فَاطِمَةُ بِنْتُ الخَطَّاب، الَّتِي كَانَتْ سَبَبًا فِي إِسْلَامِ أَخِيهَا عُمَر.

كَانَ سَعِيدٌ وَزَوْجَتُهُ مِنْ أَوَائِلِ مَنْ هَاجَرَ إِلَى الْمَدِينَةِ، وَقَدْ شَهِدَ كُلَّ الْغَزَوَاتِ إِلَّا بَدْرًا لِأَنَّهُ كَانَ فِي مَهَمَّةٍ أَوْكَلَهَا إِلَيْهِ النَّبِيّ صلى الله عليه وسلم، وَقَدْ شَهِدَ مَعْرَكَةَ الْيَرْمُوك، وَفَتْحَ دِمَشْقَ الَّتِي أَصْبَحَ وَالِيًا عَلَيْهَا.
تُوُفِّيَ رَضِيَ اللهُ عَنْهُ، سنة 51 هـ.

Sa'eed ibn Zaid was one of the first eight people to accept Islam. His wife, Fatima Bent Al-Khattab, also accepted Islam early and both were the reason Umar ibn Al-Khattab accepted Islam. He and his wife were the first to emigrate from Makkah to Madinah. He participated in all battles with the Prophet, except the Battle of Badr because he was on a mission, given to him by the Prophet, peace be upon him. He also participated in the battle of Yarmouk and the opening of Damascus. He was appointed as a governor of Damascus, and he died in the year 51 AH.

أبو عُبَيْدَة عَامِرُ بْنُ الجَرَّاحِ
Abu Abeida Amer ibn Jarrah

هُوَ أَحَدُ الْأَوَائِلِ السَّابِقِينَ إِلَى الإِسْلَامِ، لَقَّبَهُ النَّبِيُّ صلى الله عليه وسلم، بِأَمِينِ الأُمَّة. هَاجَرَ إِلَى الْحَبَشَةِ فِي الهِجْرَةِ الثَّانِيَةِ، ثُمَّ إِلَى الْمَدِينَةِ المُنَوَّرَةِ.
شَهِدَ أَبُو عُبَيْدَةَ غَزْوَةَ بَدْرٍ وَالْمَشَاهِدَ كُلَّهَا مَعَ النَّبِيِّ صلى الله عليه وسلم.
كَانَ أَبُو عُبَيْدَةُ أَحَدَ القَادَةِ الْأَرْبَعَةِ الَّذِينَ عَيَّنَهُمْ أَبُوبَكْرٍ لِفَتْحِ بِلَادِ الشَّامِ، وَقَدْ نَجَحَ أَبُو عُبَيْدَةَ فِي فَتْحِ دِمَشْق وَغَيْرِهَا مِنَ المُدن. تَوَفَّى أَبُو عُبَيْدَةَ رَضِيَ اللهُ عَنْهُ، بِسَبَبِ طَاعُون عَمَوَاس سَنَةَ 18 هـ.

Abu Abeida Amer ibn Jarrah was one of the first few to embrace Islam. He migrated to Abyssinia in the second migration and then to Madinah. He participated in all invasions with the Prophet, peace be upon him, including the Battle of Badr. The Prophet, peace be upon him, called him: "the custodian of the Ummah (nation)." He was one of the four leaders appointed by Abu Bakr to conquer Syria. He succeeded in capturing Damascus and other cities.
He was afflicted with the plague and died in the year 18 AH.

مَدْحُ الصَّحَابَةِ فِي القُرْآنِ الكَرِيم

The praises of the companions in the Qur'an

قَالَ اللهُ تَعَالَى: ﴿لَكِنِ الرَّسُولُ وَالَّذِينَ آمَنُوا مَعَهُ جَاهَدُوا بِأَمْوَالِهِمْ وَأَنْفُسِهِمْ وَأُولَئِكَ لَهُمُ الْخَيْرَاتُ وَأُولَئِكَ هُمُ الْمُفْلِحُونَ﴾ [التَّوْبة: 88].

"But, the Messenger (Muhammad) and those who believed with him (in Allah) and strived in the cause of Allah with their properties and lives; they shall have good things, and they will be successful." [9: 88].

قَالَ الحَافِظُ ابْنُ كَثِير:

(وَالصَّحَابَةُ كُلُّهُمْ عُدُولٌ عِنْدَ أَهْلِ السُّنَّةِ وَالْجَمَاعَةِ)

[الباعث الحثيث: ص 498].

Al-Haafiz Ibn Katheer said: "all the Companions are trustworthy by Ahlu-Sunnah wal-Jamaa'ah."

بِـرُّ الوَالِدَيْـنِ
Honoring Parents

قَالَ اللهُ تَعَالَى:

﴿وَقَضَىٰ رَبُّكَ أَلَّا تَعْبُدُوا إِلَّا إِيَّاهُ وَبِالْوَالِدَيْنِ إِحْسَانًا﴾

[الإسْرَاء: 23]

"Your Lord has ordered you to worship none except Him, and to be kind to your parents."

[17: 23]

بِـرُّ الْوَالِدَيْـنِ
Honoring Parents

بِرُّ الْوَالِدَيْنِ فِي الْإِسْلَامِ مِنْ أَهَمِّ الْوَاجِبَاتِ، وَقَدْ أَوْصَى اللهُ – سُبْحَانَهُ وَتَعَالَى – فِي الْقُرْآنِ الكَرِيم بِبِرِّ الْوَالِدَيْنِ وَالْإِحْسَانِ إِلَيْهِمَا. قَالَ اللهُ تَعَالَى: ﴿وَقَضَىٰ رَبُّكَ أَلَّا تَعْبُدُوا إِلَّا إِيَّاهُ وَبِالْوَالِدَيْنِ إِحْسَانًا ۚ إِمَّا يَبْلُغَنَّ عِندَكَ الْكِبَرَ أَحَدُهُمَا أَوْ كِلَاهُمَا فَلَا تَقُل لَّهُمَا أُفٍّ وَلَا تَنْهَرْهُمَا وَقُل لَّهُمَا قَوْلًا كَرِيمًا﴾. [الإسراء: 23].

وَقَالَ تَعَالَى: ﴿أَنِ اشْكُرْ لِي وَلِوَالِدَيْكَ إِلَيَّ الْمَصِيرُ﴾. [لُقْمَانُ: 14].

وَبِرُّ الْوَالِدَيْنِ مِنْ أَفْضَلِ الْأَعْمَالِ بَعْدَ الصَّلَاةِ فَفِي الصَّحِيحَيْنِ، عَنْ عَبْدِاللهِ بْنِ مَسْعُودٍ، رَضِيَ اللهُ عَنْهُ، قَالَ: سَأَلْتُ النَّبِيَّ ﷺ: أَيُّ الْعَمَلِ أَحَبُّ إِلَى اللهِ تَعَالَى؟ قَالَ: ((**الصَّلَاةُ عَلَى وَقْتِـهَا**، قُلْـتُ: ثُـمَّ أَيٌّ؟ قَالَ: **بِرُّ الْوَالِدَيْـنِ**، قُلْـتُ: ثُمَّ أَيٌّ؟ قَالَ: **الْجِهَـادُ فِي سَبِيـلِ اللهِ**))

[البُخاري وَمُسْلِمٌ].

وَاعْلَم أَنَّ بِرَّ الْوَالِدَيْنِ يَكُون فِي حَيَاتِهِما وَبَعْدَ مَوْتِهِمَا.

بِـرُّ الْوَالِدَيْنِ فِي حَيَاتِهِمَا وَيَشْمُلُ مَا يَلِي:

1. طَاعَتُهُمَا فِي كُلِّ الأُمُورِ، إِنْ لَمْ يَكُنْ فِي ذَلِكَ مَعْصِيَةً لِلهِ.
2. الْإِحْسَانُ إِلَيْهِمَا بِالْقَوْلِ وَالْفِعْلِ.
3. خَفْضُ الْجَنَاحِ لَهُمَا وَالإِصْغَاءُ لِحَدِيثِهِمَا.
4. الإِسْرَاعُ فِي مُسَاعَدَتِهِمَا فِيمَا يَحْتَاجَانِ إِلَيْه.
5. التَّوَدُّدُ إِلَيْهِمَا وَأَخْذُ مَشُورَتِهِمَا وَنَصَائِحِهِمَا.
6. الْأُمُّ، فِي الإِسْلَامِ، حَقُّهَا كَبِيرٌ وَعَظِيم.

Honoring Parents

Honoring parents is one of the most important duties in Islam. Allah has recommended, in the Holy Qur'an, to honor and respect parents. Allah said: "Your Lord has ordered you to worship none except Him, and to be kind to your parents. If either or both attain old age in your life, do not say to them a word of contempt, nor repel them, but speak to them with words of respect." [17: 23].

In another verse, Allah said: "Be grateful to Me, and your parents; to Me is the final destination." [31: 14].

Honoring parents is one of the best deeds after performing prayer on time. Abdu-Allah ibn Mas'Uod, may Allah be pleased with him, said: I asked the Prophet, peace be upon him, which deeds do Allah love? He said: "Performing prayer on time." I said, "Then what?" He said: "Honoring one's parents." I said, "Then what?" He said: "Striving for the sake of Allah." [Al-Bukhari and Muslim]. Righteousness of the parents shall be during their lifetime and after their death

Honoring parents during their life

1. Obey your parents in all matters as long as it is not disobedient to Allah.

2. Respect them and care for them by words and deeds.

3. Be humble and listen to their talk when they speak.

4. Act in haste whenever they need assistance.

5. Make them happy by accepting their counsel and advice.

6. Mothers in Islam have greater rights and are held in high regard.

بِرُّ الْوَالِدَيْنِ بَعْدَ مَوْتِهِمَا وَيَشْمَل مَا يَلِي:
Honoring Parents After Their Death

1. التَّصَدُّقُ عَنْهُمَا. عَنْ عَائِشَةَ رَضِيَ اللهُ عَنْهَا: ((أَنَّ رَجُلًا قَالَ لِلنَّبِيِّ صلى الله عليه وسلم: إِنَّ أُمِّي افْتُلِتَتْ نَفْسُهَا وَأُرَاهَا لَوْ تَكَلَّمَتْ تَصَدَّقَتْ، فَهَلْ لَهَا أَجْرٌ إِنْ تَصَدَّقْتُ عَنْهَا؟ قَالَ: **نَعَمْ**)) [البُخارِي وَمُسْلِم].

2. كَثْرَةُ الدُّعَاءِ وَالاِسْتِغْفَارِ لَهُمَا، قَالَ رَسُولُ اللهِ صلى الله عليه وسلم: ((إِذَا مَاتَ ابْنُ آدَمَ انْقَطَعَ عَمَلُهُ إِلَّا مِنْ ثَلَاثٍ: صَدَقَةٍ جَارِيَةٍ، أَوْ عِلْمٍ يُنْتَفَعُ بِهِ، أَوْ **وَلَدٍ صَالِحٍ يَدْعُو لَهُ**)) [مُسْلِم].

3. صِلَةُ أَقَارِبِهِمَا: وَهَذَا يَشْمَلُ الْإِحْسَانَ وَالزِّيَارَةَ إِلَى الْأَعْمَامِ وَالْأَخْوَالِ وَالْعَمَّاتِ وَالْخَالَاتِ.

4. قَضَاءُ مَا عَلَيْهِمَا مِنْ دُيُونٍ أَوْ أَيِّ اِلْتِزَامَاتٍ أُخْرَى.

5. إِكْرَامُ صَدِيقِهِمَا: وَهَذَا يَكُونُ بِالْإِحْسَانِ وَالزِّيَارَةِ إِلَى أَصْدِقَاءِ الْوَالِدَيْنِ بَعْدَ مَوْتِهِما.

1. Give charity on their behalf. Aisha, may Allah be pleased with her, reported: "A man said to the Prophet, peace be upon him: My mother has died suddenly. I think if she were able to speak, she would have given charity. So, if I give charity on her behalf, will she receive the reward? The Messenger of Allah, peace be upon him, said: Yes (she will get rewarded)." [Al-Bukhari and Muslim].

2. Supplicate and ask for forgiveness (from Allah) for them. The Messenger of Allah, peace be upon him, said: "If the son of Adam dies, his actions come to an end except for three: ongoing charity, beneficial knowledge, or a righteous child who prays for him." [Muslim].

3. Honor their kinship, such as uncles and aunts, through acts of kindness and by helping and visiting them.
4. Take care of your parent's unpaid debts and any other obligations.
5. Honor their friends through acts of kindness and by visiting them.

Warning – تَحْذِير

1- عُقُـوقُ الْوَالِدَيْنِ مِنَ الْكَبَائِر

Disobedience to parents is a major sin

قَالَ رَسُولُ اللهِ ﷺ: ((الْكَبَائِرُ: الإِشْرَاكُ بِاللهِ، وَعُقُوقُ الْوَالِدَيْنِ، وَقَتْلُ النَّفْسِ، وَالْيَمِينُ الْغَمُوسُ)) [البُخاري].

"The major sins are: Associating partners with Allah, disobedience to the parents, killing someone unlawfully and taking a false oath intentionally." [Al-Bukhari].

2- العَاقُّ لِوَالِدَيْهِ تُعَجَّلُ عُقُوبَتُهُ فِي الدُّنْيَا قَبْلَ الآخِرَة

Punishment for disobeying parents will be in this world before the Hereafter

قَالَ رَسُولُ اللهِ ﷺ: ((اِثْنَتَانِ يُعَجِّلُهُمَا اللهُ فِي الدُّنْيَا: الْبَغْيُ وَعُقُوقُ الْوَالِدَيْنِ.)) [صَحيحُ الجَامع (137)]

"Two things that God will speed up in this world: rebellion and disobedience to parents"

الأذْكَارُ وَالأدْعِيَةُ
Supplications

قَالَ اللهُ تَعَالَى:

﴿وَقَالَ رَبُّكُمُ ادْعُونِي أَسْتَجِبْ لَكُمْ﴾

[غافِر: 60]

"And your Lord said; call upon Me and I shall respond to you." [40: 60]

أَهَمِّيَةُ الدُّعَاء
The Importance of Ssupplications

الدُّعَاءُ هُوَ مُنَاجَاةُ العَبْدِ لِرَبِّهِ، وَهُوَ عِبادَةٌ عَظِيمَةٌ. قَالَ ﷺ: ((الدُّعَاءُ هُوَ العِبَادَةُ)) [أحمد وأصحاب السُّنن].

فَالدُّعَاء - الإِلْتِجَاءُ إِلَى اللهِ - يَجْلِبُ لِلْعَبْدِ الخَيْرَ وَالأَجْرَ وَالثَّوَاب وَيَدْفَعُ عَنْهُ الشَّر.

الدُّعَاءُ مُسْتَحَبٌّ فِي جَمِيعِ الْأَوْقَاتِ وَالْأَحْوَالِ فَعَلَى المُسْلِمِ أَنْ يَسْأَلَ اللهَ وَيَدْعُوهُ بِأَسْمَائِهِ الحُسْنَى وَصِفَاتِهِ العُلَا.

قَالَ تَعَالَى: ﴿وَلِلَّهِ الْأَسْمَاءُ الْحُسْنَى فَادْعُوهُ﴾ [الأعراف: 180].

وَقَالَ تَعَالَى: ﴿وَقَالَ رَبُّكُمُ ادْعُونِي أَسْتَجِبْ لَكُمْ﴾ [غافر: 60].

فِي هَذَا الفَصْلِ سَنَذْكُرُ بَعْضَ الأَدْعِيَةِ الَّتِي وَرَدَتْ فِي الْقُرْآنِ الْكَرِيمِ وَالسُّنَّةِ الصَّحِيحَةِ لِرَسُولِ اللهِ، ﷺ.

Supplication is a great worship of the slave to his Lord. The Prophet, peace be upon him, said: "Supplication is worship." [Ahmad and Ashab Asunan]. The supplication of the slave to his Lord (Allah) brings good benefits, big rewards, and saves against the evil deeds. Supplication is desirable at all times. A Muslim should direct his supplication to Almighty Allah, by invoking His Excellent Names and His High Attributes.
Allah said: "To Allah belong the most beautiful names, so call on Him by them." [7: 180]. In another verse, Allah said: "And your Lord said, call Me, and I shall respond to you." [40: 60].
In this chapter, you will find some supplications, that mentioned in the Nobel Qur'an and in the Sunnah of the Prophet, peace be upon him.

أدْعِيَةٌ مِنَ الْقُرْآنِ الْكَرِيم

Supplications from the Noble Qur'an

﴿رَبَّنَا تَقَبَّلْ مِنَّا إِنَّكَ أَنتَ السَّمِيعُ الْعَلِيم﴾

[البَقَرة: 127].

"Our Lord! (Allah); Accept from us (our deeds). Verily, you are the All-Hearer, the All-Knower." [2: 127].

﴿رَّبَّنَا عَلَيْكَ تَوَكَّلْنَا وَإِلَيْكَ أَنبْنَا وَإِلَيْكَ الْمَصِيرُ﴾

[المُمْتَحِنة: 4]

"Our Lord, upon You (alone) we have relied, to You we turn in repentance, and to You is (our) destination." [60: 4]

﴿رَبَّنَا لاَ تُزِغْ قُلُوبَنَا بَعْدَ إِذْ هَدَيْتَنَا وَهَبْ لَنَا مِن لَّدُنكَ رَحْمَةً إِنَّكَ أَنتَ الْوَهَّابُ﴾ [آلِ عِمران: 8].

"Our Lord! (Allah); Let our hearts, not go astray, after You guided us, and grant us Your Mercy; indeed, You are the Bestower." [2: 8].

﴿ رَبَّنَا آتِنَا مِن لَّدُنكَ رَحْمَةً وَهَيِّئْ لَنَا مِنْ أَمْرِنَا رَشَدًا ﴾

[الكَهف: 10].

"Our Lord! (Allah); Have mercy on us from You, and prepare for us good guidance in all our affairs." [18: 10].

﴿رَبَّنَا آمَنَّا بِمَا أَنزَلْتَ وَاتَّبَعْنَا الرَّسُولَ فَاكْتُبْنَا مَعَ الشَّاهِدِينَ﴾ [آلِ عِمران: 53]

"Our Lord! (Allah); We believe in what You have revealed, and we follow the Messenger (Muhammad); then write us down among those who bear witness." [3:53].

﴿رَبَّنَا آمَنَّا فَاغْفِرْ لَنَا وَارْحَمْنَا وَأَنتَ خَيْرُ الرَّاحِمِينَ﴾

[المُؤمِنون: 109].

"Our Lord! (Allah); We have believed, so forgive us and have mercy upon us, and You are the best of the merciful." [23: 109].

﴿رَبَّنَا اغْفِرْ لَنَا وَلِإِخْوَانِنَا الَّذِينَ سَبَقُونَا بِالْإِيمَانِ وَلَا تَجْعَلْ فِي قُلُوبِنَا غِلًّا لِّلَّذِينَ آمَنُوا رَبَّنَا إِنَّكَ رَءُوفٌ رَّحِيمٌ﴾

[الحَشر: 10].

"Our Lord! (Allah); Forgive us and our brothers, who preceded us by faith and leave not in our hearts any hatred to those who believed. Our Lord, you are indeed the Most Kind and the Most Merciful." [59: 10].

﴿رَبَّنَا اغْفِرْ لِي وَلِوَالِدَيَّ وَلِلْمُؤْمِنِينَ يَوْمَ يَقُومُ الْحِسَابُ﴾

[إبْراهِيم: 41].

"Our Lord! (Allah); Forgive me, my parents, and the believers on the Day of accountability." [14: 41].

﴿رَبِّ أَوْزِعْنِي أَنْ أَشْكُرَ نِعْمَتَكَ الَّتِي أَنْعَمْتَ عَلَيَّ وَعَلَى وَالِدَيَّ وَأَنْ أَعْمَلَ صَالِحًا تَرْضَاهُ وَأَصْلِحْ لِي فِي ذُرِّيَّتِي إِنِّي تُبْتُ إِلَيْكَ وَإِنِّي مِنَ الْمُسْلِمِينَ﴾ [الأحقاف: 15].

"**O My Lord!** grant me that I should be grateful for Your, which bestowed upon me and upon my parents, and that I do good deeds that please You, and make good in my offspring. I have repented to you, and I am one of the Muslims." [46: 15].

﴿حَسْبِيَ اللهُ لَا إِلَٰهَ إِلَّا هُوَ عَلَيْهِ تَوَكَّلْتُ وَهُوَ رَبُّ الْعَرْشِ الْعَظِيمِ﴾ [التَّوْبة: 129].

"**Allah** (alone) is sufficient for me. There is no god but He. On Him, I rely, and He is the Lord of the Great Throne." [9:129].

﴿لَا إِلَٰهَ إِلَّا أَنْتَ سُبْحَانَكَ إِنِّي كُنْتُ مِنَ الظَّالِمِينَ﴾

[الأنْبِياء: 87]

"There is no god except You (O Allah);
All glory be to You; Indeed, I have been of the wrongdoers." [21: 87]

﴿رَبَّنَا أَفْرِغْ عَلَيْنَا صَبْرًا وَتَوَفَّنَا مُسْلِمِينَ﴾

[الأعراف:126]

"**Our Lord!** Grant us patience and let us die as Muslims." [7: 126].

أَدْعِيَةٌ مِنَ السُّنَّة
Supplications from the Sunnah

The Master of Forgiveness – سَيِّدُ الإسْتِغْفار

((اللَّهُمَّ أَنْتَ رَبِّي لَّا إِلٰهَ إِلَّا أَنْتَ، خَلَقْتَنِي وَأَنَا عَبْدُكَ، وَأَنَا عَلَى عَهْدِكَ وَوَعْدِكَ مَا اسْتَطَعْتُ، أَعُوذُ بِكَ مِنْ شَرِّ مَا صَنَعْتُ، أَبُوءُ لَكَ بِنِعْمَتِكَ عَلَيَّ، وَأَبُوءُ بِذَنْبِي فَاغْفِرْ لِي فَإِنَّهُ لَا يَغْفِرُ الذُّنُوبَ إِلَّا أَنْتَ)) [رَواهُ البُخارِي].

"**O Allah!** You are my Lord. None has the right to be worshipped except You. You created me, and I am Your slave, and I am keeping Your covenant and promise as best as I can, I seek refuge in You from the evil of the wrong that I have done. I acknowledge Your Blessings and favors upon me, and I acknowledge my sin, so forgive me, for none forgives sins except You." [Al-Bukhari].

The Best Supplication – خَيْرُ الدُّعَاءِ

((لَا إِلٰـهَ إِلاَّ اللهُ وَحْدَهُ لاَ شَرِيكَ لَهُ، لَهُ المُلْكُ وَلَهُ الحَمْدُ؛ وَهُوَ عَلَى كُلِّ شَيْءٍ قَدِيرٌ)) [رَواهُ البُخارِي ومُسْلم].

"**There is no god but Allah.** He is One and has no partner. All the kingdom and all praises are His; He has all the power to do anything." [Al-Bukhari and Muslim].

Qunut Supplication - دُعَاءُ الْقُنُوت

((اللَّهُمَّ اهْدِنِي فِيمَنْ هَدَيْتَ، وَعَافِنِي فِيمَنْ عَافَيْتَ، وَتَوَلَّنِي فِيمَنْ تَوَلَّيْتَ، وَبَارِكْ لِي فِيمَا أَعْطَيْتَ، وَقِنِي شَرَّ مَا قَضَيْتَ، إِنَّكَ تَقْضِي وَلَا يُقْضَى عَلَيْكَ، وَإِنَّهُ لَا يَذِلُّ مَنْ وَالَيْتَ، وَلَا يَعِزُّ مَنْ عَادَيْتَ، تَبَارَكْتَ رَبَّنَا وَتَعَالَيْتَ، وَلَا مَنْجَا مِنْكَ إِلَّا إِلَيْكَ)) [رَواهُ أبو داود والتّرمذي وحسّنه]

"**O Allah,** guide me among those You have guided, grant me security with those You have granted security, Take charge of me and make me with those You have taken charge of them, bless what You have given me, guard me from the evil of what You hast decreed, for You decree, and no one can decree for You. He whom You have taken care of is never disgraced; he whom You have made an enemy shall never find honor. Blessed and Exalted High are You, our Lord." [Abu Dawud and At-Tirmidhi].

((اللَّهُمَّ إِنِّي أَعُوذُ بِرِضَاكَ مِنْ سَخَطِكَ، وَأَعُوذُ بِمُعَافَاتِكَ مِنْ عُقُوبَتِكَ، وَأَعُوذُ بِكَ مِنْكَ، لَا أُحْصِي ثَنَاءً عَلَيْكَ، أَنْتَ كَمَا أَثْنَيْتَ عَلَى نَفْسِكَ)) [رَواه مُسْلِم].

"**My Lord!** I seek refuge from Your anger in Your mercy, from Your punishment in Your forgiveness; I seek refuge from You in You. I am unable to find enough words of praise for You. You are as You have praised Yourself to be." [Muslim].

((اللَّـهُمَّ اقْسِمْ لَنَا مِنْ خَشْيَتِكَ مَا تَحُولُ بِهِ بَيْنَنَا وَبَيْنَ مَعَاصِيكَ، وَمِنْ طَاعَتِكَ مَا تُبَلِّغُنَا بِهِ جَنَّتَكَ، وَمِنَ الْيَقِينِ مَا تُهَوِّنُ بِهِ عَلَيْنَا مَصَائِبَ الدُّنْيَا، اللَّـهُمَّ مَتِّعْنَا بِأَسْمَاعِنَا، وَأَبْصَارِنَا، وَقُوَّاتِنَا مَا أَحْيَيْتَنَا، وَاجْعَلْهُ الْوَارِثَ مِنَّا، وَاجْعَلْ ثَأْرَنَا عَلَى مَنْ ظَلَمَنَا، وَانْصُرْنَا عَلَى مَنْ عَادَانَا، وَلَا تَجْعَلْ مُصِيبَتَنَا فِي دِينِنَا، وَلَا تَجْعَلِ الدُّنْيَا أَكْبَرَ هَمِّنَا، وَلَا مَبْلَغَ عِلْمِنَا، وَلَا تُسَلِّطْ عَلَيْنَا مَنْ لَا يَرْحَمُنَا)) [رَواهُ التِّرمذي والنّسائي].

"O Allah, apportion for us, reverential fear of You, that shall come between us and disobedience of You; and of obedience to You, which shall cause us to obtain Your Paradise; and of certainty, which shall make the afflictions of the world easy for us; and enjoyment of our hearing, and our seeing, and our strength as long as You keep us alive; and make it the inheritor of us. And let our vengeance be upon those who have wronged us; and aid us against those who show enmity towards us; and do not make our affliction in our religion; and do not make this world our greatest concern, nor the limit of our knowledge; and do not give power over us to those who will not have mercy on us." [At-Tirmidhi and An- Nasa'i].

((اللَّـهُمَّ رَبَّ النَّاسِ، أَذْهِبِ الْبَأسَ، واشْفِ، أَنْتَ الشَّافِي، لَا شِفَاءَ إِلَّا شِفَاؤُكَ، شِفَاءً لَا يُغَادِرُ سَقَمًا)) [رَواهُ البُخاري ومُسْلِم].

"O Allah, the Lord of the people, take away the harm and heal, You are the Healer, no healing except Your healing, and healing that does not leave illness." [Al-Bukhari and Muslim].

((اللَّهُمَّ إنِّي أَسْأَلُكَ الْجَنَّةَ وَأَسْتَجِيرُ بِكَ مِنَ النَّارِ))

[رواه التّرمذي وابن ماجه والنّسائي].

"**O Allah,** I ask You Paradise, and I seek refuge in You from the Fire." [At-Tirmidhi, Ibn Majah, and An-Nasa'i].

((اللَّهُمَّ إِنِّي ظَلَمْتُ نَفْسِي ظُلْمًا كَثِيرًا وَلَا يَغْفِرُ الذُّنُوبَ إِلَّا أَنْتَ فَاغْفِرْ لِي مَغْفِرَةً مِنْ عِنْدِكَ وَارْحَمْنِي إِنَّكَ أَنْتَ الْغَفُورُ الرَّحِيمُ)) [رَواهُ البُخارِي ومُسْلِم].

"**O Allah,** I have wronged myself so much injustice, and I will not forgive sins except You. Forgive me forgiveness from you and have mercy on me. You are the Forgiving, the Merciful." [Al-Bukhari and Muslim].

((اللَّهُمَّ أَسْلَمْتُ نَفْسِي إِلَيْكَ، وَوَجَّهْتُ وَجْهِي إِلَيْكَ. وَفَوَّضتُ أَمْرِي إِلَيْكَ، وَأَلجَأْتُ ظَهْرِي إِلَيْكَ، رَغْبَةً ورَهْبَةً إِلَيْكَ، لامَلْجأَ وَلَا مَنْجى مِنْكَ إِلَّا إِلَيْكَ، آمَنْتُ بِكِتَابِكَ الّذِي أَنزَلْت، وَبِنَبِيِّكَ الّذِي أَرْسَلتَ)) [رَواهُ البُخارِي ومُسْلِم].

"**O Allah!** I have submitted myself to You, I have turned my face to You, I entrusted my affairs to You, and depend on You for protection out of desire for You and out of fear of You (expecting Your reward and fearing Your punishment). There is neither refuge nor a place of safety from You except with You. I believed in the Book [Qur'an] You have revealed, and in the Prophet (Muhammad) You have sent." [Al-Bukhari and Muslim].

الحَـدِيـث

Al-Hadith

قَالَ صلى الله عليه وسلم :

((نَضَّرَ اللهُ اِمْرَأً سَمِعَ مَقَالَتِي فَوَعَاهَا وَحَفِظَهَا وَبَلَّغَهَا))

"May Allah make his face bright, whoever heard what I had said then learned, memorized, and communicated it to others as it is ..."

[رَواه التّرمذي وأحمد]

[1] - الحَدِيثُ الأوَّلُ

عَنْ أَمِيرِ الْمُؤْمِنِينَ أَبِي حَفْصٍ عُمَرَ بْنِ الْخَطَّابِ، رَضِيَ اللهُ عَنْهُ، قَالَ: سَمِعْتُ رَسُولَ اللهِ ﷺ، يَقُولُ:

((إِنَّمَا الأَعْمَالُ بِالنِّيَّاتِ، وَإِنَّمَا لِكُلِّ امْرِئٍ مَا نَوَى، فَمَنْ كَانَتْ هِجْرَتُهُ إِلَى اللهِ وَرَسُولِهِ فَهِجْرَتُهُ إِلَى اللهِ وَرَسُولِهِ، وَمَنْ كَانَتْ هِجْرَتُهُ لِدُنْيَا يُصِيبُهَا أَوِ امْرَأَةٍ يَنْكِحُهَا فَهِجْرَتُهُ إِلَى مَا هَاجَرَ إِلَيْهِ)) [رَواهُ البُخارِي ومُسْلِم].

The commander of the believers Umar ibn Al-Khattab, may Allah be pleased with him, said: I heard the Messenger of Allah, Peace be upon him, saying:

"Actions are (judged) **by intentions, and everyone rewarded according to his intention. Whoever has emigrated for Allah and His Messenger, his emigration will be for Allah and His Messenger; and whoever has emigrated for worldly benefit or to marry a woman, then his emigration is for what he had emigrated for"** [Narrated by Al-Bukhari and Muslim].

[2] - الحَدِيثُ الثَّانِي

عَنْ عُثْمَانَ بْنِ عَفَّانَ، رَضِيَ اللهُ عَنْهُ، قَالَ: قَالَ رَسُولُ اللهِ ﷺ:

((مَنْ مَاتَ وَهُوَ يَعْلَمُ أَنَّهُ لَا إِلَهَ إِلَّا اللهُ دَخَلَ الْجَنَّةَ)) [رَواهُ مُسْلِم].

Uthman, may Allah be pleased with him, said: The Messenger of Allah, peace be upon him, said:

"Whoever dies knowing there is no god has the right to be worshipped but Allah, he will enter Paradise."
[Narrated by Muslim].

[3] – الحَدِيثُ الثَّالِثُ

عَنْ أَبِي هُرَيْرَةَ، رَضِـيَ اللهُ عَنْهُ، قَالَ: سَمِعْتُ رَسُولَ اللهِ صلى الله عليه وسلم، يَقُولُ: ((**قَالَ اللهُ تَعَالَى: أَنَا أَغْنَى الشُّرَكَاءِ عَنِ الشِّرْكِ، مَنْ عَمِلَ عَمَلًا أَشْرَكَ فِيهِ مَعِي غَيْرِي، تَرَكْتُهُ وَشِرْكَهُ**)) [رَوَاهُ مُسْلِم].

Abu Hurairah, may Allah be pleased with him, said: I heard the Messenger of Allah, peace be upon him, saying:
"Almighty Allah said: I am self-sufficient and in no need of having partners. He who does a thing for the sake of someone besides Me, I discard him and his polytheism." [Narrated by Muslim].

[4] – الحَدِيثُ الرَّابِعُ

عَنْ أُمِّ المُؤْمِنِينَ، أُمِّ عَبْدِ اللهِ، عَائِشَةَ، رَضِـيَ اللهُ عَنْهَا، قَالَتْ: قَالَ رَسُولُ اللهِ صلى الله عليه وسلم: ((**مَنْ أَحْدَثَ فِي أَمْرِنَا هَذَا مَا لَيْسَ مِنْهُ فَهُوَ رَدٌّ**)) [رَوَاهُ البُخَارِي ومُسْلِم].

وَفِي رِوَايَةٍ لِمُسْلِم: ((**مَنْ عَمِلَ عَمَلًا لَيْسَ عَلَيْهِ أَمْرُنَا فَهُوَ رَدٌّ**))

The mother of the believers, Aisha, may Allah be pleased with her, reported that: The Messenger of Allah, Peace be upon him, said: **"Whoever introduces to our matter** (religion) **something that does not belong to it, it will be rejected."** [Al-Bukhari and Muslim].

The one reported by Muslim says:
"Whoever practices something that is not according to our matter (religion)**, will be rejected."**

[5] – الحَدِيثُ الخَامِسُ

عَنْ عَبْدِاللهِ بْنِ عُمَرَ، رَضِـيَ اللهُ عَنْـهُمَا، قَالَ: قَالَ رَسُولُ اللهِ ﷺ:

((بُنِيَ الإِسْلَامُ عَلَى خَمْسٍ: شَهَادَةِ أَنْ لَا إِلَـهَ إِلَّا اللهُ، وَأَنَّ مُحَمَّـدًا رَسُولُ اللهِ، وَإِقَامِ الصَّلَاةِ، وَإِيتَاءِ الزَّكَاةِ، وَحَجِّ الْبَيْتِ، وَصَوْمِ رَمَضَانَ)) [رَواهُ البُخارِي ومُسْلِم].

Ibn Umar, may Allah be pleased with them, said: The Messenger of Allah, peace be upon him, said:
"Islam built on five pillars: testifying that there is no god but Allah, Muhammad is the Messenger of Allah, performing the prayer, paying Zakah (obligatory charity), **performing pilgrimage to the House of Allah, and fasting the month of Ramadan."**
[Narrated by Al-Bukhari and Muslim].

[6] – الحَدِيثُ السَّادِسُ

عَنْ أَبِي هُرَيْرَةَ، رَضِـيَ اللهُ عَنْـهُ، أَنَّ رَسُولَ اللهِ ﷺ، كَانَ يَقُولُ:

((الصَّلَوَاتُ الْخَمْسُ، وَالْجُمُعَةُ إِلَى الْجُمُعَةِ، وَرَمَضَانُ إِلَى رَمَضَانَ، مُكَفِّرَاتٌ لِمَا بَيْنَهُـنَّ إِذَا اجْتُنِبَتِ الْكَبَائِرُ))

[رَواهُ مُسْلِم].

Abu Hurairah, may Allah be pleased with him, reported that: The Messenger of Allah, peace be upon him, was saying:
"The five daily prayers and Friday to Friday and Ramadan to Ramadan is an expiation of sins to whom avoid major sins." [Narrated by Muslim].

[7] – الحَدِيثُ السَّابِعُ

عَنْ أَبِي هُرَيْـرَةَ، رَضِـيَ اللهُ عَنْهُ، أَنَّ رَسُولَ اللهِ صلى الله عليه وسلم قَالَ:

((الْعُمْـرَةُ إِلَى الْعُمْـرَةِ كَفَّارَةٌ لِمَا بَيْنَهُمَا، وَالْحَجُّ الْمَبْـرُورُ لَيْسَ لَهُ جَزَاءٌ إِلَّا الْجَنَّـةُ))

[رَواهُ البُخارِي ومُسْلِم].

Abu Hurairah, may Allah be pleased with him, reported that: The Messenger of Allah, peace be upon him, said: **"Umrah** (minor pilgrimage) **to the next Umrah is an expiation of the sins committed in between, and the reward of accepted Hajj is nothing but Paradise."** [Narrated by Al-Bukhari and Muslim].

[8] – الحَدِيثُ الثَّامِنُ

عَنْ أَبِي سَعِيدٍ الخُدْرِيِّ، رَضِـيَ اللهُ عَنْهُ، قَالَ: سَمِعْتُ رَسُولَ اللهِ صلى الله عليه وسلم يَقُولُ:

((مَـنْ رَأَى مِنْكُمْ مُنْكَـرًا فَلْيُغَيِّرْهُ بِيَـدِهِ، فَإِنْ لَمْ يَسْتَطِعْ فَبِلِسَانِهِ، فَإِنْ لَمْ يَسْتَطِعْ فَبِقَلْبِهِ وَذَلِكَ أَضْعَفُ الْإِيمَانِ))

[رَوَاهُ مُسْلِم].

Abu Sa`id Al-Khudri, may Allah be pleased with him, reported that: The Messenger of Allah, peace be upon him, said: **"Whoever among you, who sees an evil act must change it with his hand; if he cannot do so, then with his tongue; and if he cannot do so, then with his heart; and that is the weakest form of faith."** [Narrated by Muslim].

[9] – الحَدِيثُ التَّاسِعُ

عَنْ أَبِي هُرَيْـرَةَ، رَضِـيَ اللهُ عَنْـهُ، أَنَّ رَسُولَ اللهِ ﷺ قَالَ:

((كُلُّ أُمَّتِي يَدْخُلُونَ الْجَنَّةَ إِلَّا مَنْ أَبَى، قَالُوا: يَا رَسُولَ اللهِ وَمَنْ يَأْبَى؟ قَالَ: **مَنْ أَطَاعَنِي دَخَلَ الْجَنَّـةَ، وَمَنْ عَصَانِي فَقَـدْ أَبَى))**

[رَواهُ البُخارِي].

Abu Hurairah, may Allah be pleased with him, reported that: The Messenger of Allah, peace be upon him, said:
"All my Ummah (nation) **will enter Paradise, except those who refuse,** they said: O Messenger of Allah! Who will refuse? He said: **"Whoever obeys me will enter Paradise and whoever disobeys me, he refuses** (to enter Paradise)."
[Narrated by Al-Bukhari].

[10] – الحَدِيثُ العَاشِرُ

عَنْ أَنَسِ بْنِ مَالِكٍ، رَضِـيَ اللهُ عَنْهُ، عَنِ النَّبِيِّ ﷺ قَالَ:

((لَا يُؤْمِنُ أَحَدُكُـمْ حَتَّى أَكُونَ أَحَـبَّ إِلَيْـهِ مِـنْ وَالِدِهِ، وَوَلَدِهِ، وَالنَّاسِ أَجْمَعِينَ))

[رَواهُ البُخارِي ومُسْلِم].

Anas, may Allah be pleased with him, reported that: The Prophet, peace be upon him, said:
"None of you believes until I am dearer to him than his father, his son, and all the people."
[Narrated by Al-Bukhari and Muslim].

[11] - الحَدِيثُ الحَادِي عَشَرَ

عَنْ عَبْدِاللهِ بْنِ عَمْرِو بْنِ الْعَاصِ، رَضِيَ اللهُ عَنْهُمَا، قَالَ: قَالَ رَسُولُ اللهِ ﷺ:

((الْمُسْلِمُ مَنْ سَلِمَ الْمُسْلِمُونَ مِنْ لِسَانِهِ وَيَدِهِ، وَالْمُهَاجِرُ مَنْ هَجَرَ مَا نَهَى اللهُ عَنْهُ)) [رَوَاهُ البُخارِي ومُسْلِم].

Abdullah ibn Amar, may Allah be pleased with him, reported that: The Messenger of Allah, peace be upon him, said: **"A Muslim is the one who does not harm Muslims with his tongue and or his hand. And an immigrant is the one who does not do what Allah has forbidden."**
[Narrated by Al-Bukhari and Muslim].

[12] - الحَدِيثُ الثّانِي عَشَرَ

عَنْ أَبِي مُوسَى الْأَشْعَرِيِّ، رَضِيَ اللهُ عَنْهُ، عَنِ النَّبِيِّ ﷺ قَالَ:

((إِنَّ اللهَ تَعَالَى يَبْسُطُ يَدَهُ بِاللَّيْلِ لِيَتُوبَ مُسِيءُ النَّهَارِ، وَيبْسُطُ يَدَهُ بِالنَّهَارِ لِيَتُوبَ مُسِيءُ اللَّيْلِ، حَتَّى تَطْلُعَ الشَّمْسُ مِنْ مَغْرِبِهَا)) [رَوَاهُ مُسْلِم].

Abu Musa Al-Ash'ari, may Allah be pleased with him, reported that: The Prophet, peace be upon him, said: **"Verily, the Almighty Allah, stretches out His Hand at night, so that the sinners of the day may repent, and stretches out His Hand during the day so that the sinners of the night may repent. He continually does so until the sun rises from the west."** [Narrated by Muslim].

[13] - الحَدِيثُ الثَّالِث عَشَرَ

عَنْ أَنَسِ بْنِ مَالِكٍ، رَضِـيَ اللهُ عَنْهُ، أنَّ رَسُولَ اللهِ ﷺ قَالَ:

((مَـنْ أَحَـبَّ أَنْ يُبْسَـطَ لَهُ فِي رِزْقِـهِ، وَيُنْسَأَ لَهُ فِي أَثَّـرِهِ، فَلْيَصِـلْ رَحِمَـهُ))

[رَواهُ البُخارِي ومُسْلِم].

Anas, may Allah be pleased with him, reported that: The Messenger of Allah, peace be upon him, said:
"Whoever would like to increase his provisions and prolong his life, he should have good ties with his kin."

[Narrated by Al-Bukhari and Muslim].

[14] - الحَدِيثُ السَادِسَ عَشَرَ

عَنْ أَنَسِ بْنِ مَالِكٍ، رَضِـيَ اللهُ عَنْهُ، عَنِ النَّبِيِّ ﷺ قَالَ:

((يَسِّـرُوا وَلَا تُعَسِّـرُوا، وَبَشِّـرُوا وَلَا تُنَفِّـرُوا))

[رَواهُ البُخارِي ومُسْلِم].

Anas, may Allah be pleased with him, reported that: The Prophet, peace be upon him said:
"Facilitate things and do not make them difficult. Give people glad tidings and do not be repulsed."

[Narrated by Al-Bukhari and Muslim].

[15] – الحَدِيثُ الخَامِسَ عَشَرَ

عَنْ عَبْدِاللهِ بْنِ عَمْرِو بْنِ الْعَاصِ، رَضِيَ اللهُ عنْهُمَا، قَالَ: قَال رَسُولُ اللَّـهِ صلى الله عليه وسلم:

((اللَّهُمَّ مُصَرِّفَ الْقُلُوبِ صَرِّفْ قُلُوبَنَا عَلَى طَاعَتِكَ))

[رَوَاهُ مُسْلِم].

Abdullah ibn Amr ibn Al-Aas, may Allah be pleased with him, said: The Messenger of Allah, peace be upon him, said: **"O Allah, You control the hearts, direct our hearts to Your obedience."**

[Narrated by Muslim].

[16] – الحَدِيثُ الرَّابِعَ عَشَرَ

عَنْ أَبِي هُرَيْرَةَ، رَضِيَ اللهُ عَنْهُ، قَالَ: قَالَ رَسُولُ اللهِ صلى الله عليه وسلم:

((إِذَا مَاتَ ابْنُ آدَمَ انْقَطَعَ عَمَلُهُ إِلَّا مِنْ ثَلَاثٍ: صَدَقَةٍ جَارِيَةٍ، أَوْ عِلْمٍ يُنْتَفَعُ بِهِ، أَوْ وَلَدٍ صَالِحٍ يَدْعُو لَهُ)) [رَوَاهُ مُسْلِم].

Abu Hurairah, may Allah be pleased with him, said: The Messenger of Allah, peace be upon him, said:
"If the son of Adam dies, then his actions come to an end except for three: ongoing charity, beneficial knowledge, or a righteous child who prays for him. [Narrated by Muslim].

[17] – الحَدِيثُ السَّابِعَ عَشَرَ

عَنْ عُمَرَ بْنِ الْخَطَّابِ، رَضِيَ اللهُ عَنْهُ، قَالَ: "بَيْنَمَا نَحْنُ جُلُوسٌ عِنْدَ رَسُولِ اللهِ صلى الله عليه وسلم ذَاتَ يَوْمٍ، إِذْ طَلَعَ عَلَيْنَا رَجُلٌ شَدِيدُ بَيَاضِ الثِّيَابِ، شَدِيدُ سَوَادِ الشَّعْرِ، لَا يُرَى عَلَيْهِ أَثَرُ السَّفَرِ، وَلَا يَعْرِفُهُ مِنَّا أَحَدٌ، حَتَّى جَلَسَ إِلَى النَّبِيِّ صلى الله عليه وسلم، فَأَسْنَدَ رُكْبَتَيْهِ إِلَى رُكْبَتَيْهِ، وَوَضَعَ كَفَّيْهِ عَلَى فَخِذَيْهِ، وَقَالَ: يَا مُحَمَّدُ أَخْبِرْنِي عَنِ الْإِسْلَامِ، فَقَالَ رَسُولُ اللهِ صلى الله عليه وسلم: **(الْإِسْلَامُ أَنْ تَشْهَدَ أَنْ لَا إِلَهَ إِلَّا اللهُ وَأَنَّ مُحَمَّدًا رَسُولُ اللهِ، وَتُقِيمَ الصَّلَاةَ، وَتُؤْتِيَ الزَّكَاةَ، وَتَصُومَ رَمَضَانَ، وَتَحُجَّ الْبَيْتَ إِنِ اسْتَطَعْتَ إِلَيْهِ سَبِيلًا)** قَالَ: صَدَقْتَ. فَعَجِبْنَا لَهُ يَسْأَلُهُ وَيُصَدِّقُهُ. قَالَ: فَأَخْبِرْنِي عَنِ الْإِيمَانِ، قَالَ: **(أَنْ تُؤْمِنَ بِاللهِ، وَمَلَائِكَتِهِ، وَكُتُبِهِ، وَرُسُلِهِ، وَالْيَوْمِ الْآخِرِ، وَتُؤْمِنَ بِالْقَدَرِ خَيْرِهِ وَشَرِّهِ)** قَالَ: صَدَقْتَ. قَالَ فَأَخْبِرْنِي عَنِ الْإِحْسَانِ. قَالَ: **(أَنْ تَعْبُدَ اللهَ كَأَنَّكَ تَرَاهُ، فَإِنْ لَمْ تَكُنْ تَرَاهُ فَإِنَّهُ يَرَاكَ)**. قَالَ: فَأَخْبِرْنِي عَنِ السَّاعَةِ قَالَ: **(مَا الْمَسْئُولُ عَنْهَا بِأَعْلَمَ مِنَ السَّائِلِ)**. قَالَ: فَأَخْبِرْنِي عَنْ أَمَارَاتِهَا. قَالَ: **(أَنْ تَلِدَ الْأَمَةُ رَبَّتَهَا، وَأَنْ تَرَى الْحُفَاةَ الْعُرَاةَ الْعَالَةَ رِعَاءَ الشَّاءِ يَتَطَاوَلُونَ فِي الْبُنْيَانِ)** قَالَ: ثُمَّ انْطَلَقَ فَلَبِثْتُ مَلِيًّا ثُمَّ قَالَ: (يَا عُمَرُ! أَتَدْرِي مَنِ السَّائِلُ؟) قُلْتُ: اللهُ وَرَسُولُهُ أَعْلَمُ. قَالَ: **(فَإِنَّهُ جِبْرِيلُ أَتَاكُمْ يُعَلِّمُكُمْ دِينَكُمْ).**" [رَوَاهُ مُسْلِم].

Umar ibn Al-Khattab, may Allah be pleased with him, reported that: One day while we were sitting with Allah's Messenger, peace be upon him, a man appeared before us with very white clothes and very black hair. No signs of travel shown on him and none of us knew him. He sat down by the Prophet and rested his knees over his thighs, and he said: "O Muhammad! Tell me about Islam." The Messenger of Allah said: "Islam is to testify that there is no deity worthy of worship except Allah and that Muhammad is the Messenger of Allah, to perform the prayer, to pay the Zakah (charity – poor-due), to fast during Ramadan, and to perform Hajj (pilgrimage) to the House (of Allah, the Ka`bah at Makkah), if you are able to do so." He said: "You have spoken the truth." We were astonished at him, he (the man) asking the Prophet and then telling him that he was right. Then he said: "tell me about Iman (faith). " The Prophet said: " you believe in Allah, His angels, His Books, His Messengers, in the Last Day, and to believe in the Qadr (divine destiny), both in its good and in its bad aspects." He said: "You have spoken the truth." Then the man said, "Tell me about Ihsaan." He (the Prophet) said: "It is that you worship Allah as you see Him, but you cannot see Him, yet He (Allah) sees you." Then the man said: "Tell me about the Hour (Day of Judgment). "The Prophet said: "The one questioned knows no better than the questioner." Then he said: "Tell me about its signs." He said: "When the slave-girl will give birth to her mistress, and you will see the barefooted ones, the naked, the destitute, the herdsmen of the sheep competing in raising tall buildings." Then the man went away. I waited for a while, and then the Prophet said: "O Umar, do you know who the questioner was?" I said: "Allah and His Messenger know best." He said: "That was Gabriel. He came to teach you your religion." [Narrated by Muslim].

[18] – الحَدِيثُ الثَامِنَ عَشَرَ

عَنْ عَبْدِاللهِ بْنِ عَمْرِو بْنِ الْعَاصِ، رَضِـيَ اللهُ عَنْهُمَا، عَنِ النَّبِيِّ صلى الله عليه وسلم قَالَ:

((الْكَبَائِـرُ: الْإِشْـرَاكُ بِاللهِ، وَعُقُوقُ الْوَالِدَيْـنِ، وقَتْـلُ النَّفْسِ، والْيَمِينُ الْغَمُوسُ))

[رَوَاهُ البُخَارِي].

Abdullah ibn Amr ibn Al-As, may Allah be pleased with them, reported that: The Prophet, peace be upon him, said: **"The major sins are: to ascribe partners to Allah, to disobey parents, to murder someone, and to take a false oath** (intentionally)**."** [Narrated by Al-Bukhari].

[19] – الحَدِيثُ التَّاسِعَ عَشَرَ

عَنْ أَبِي مَسْعُودٍ الأَنْصَارِيِّ الْبَدْرِيِّ، رَضِـيَ اللهُ عَنْهُ، قَالَ: قَالَ رَسُولُ اللهِ ﷺ:

((مَـنْ دَلَّ عَلَى خَيْـرٍ فَلَهُ مِثْـلُ أَجْـرِ فَاعِلِهِ))

[رَوَاهُ مُسْلِم].

Abu Mas'ud al-Ansari al-Badri, may Allah be pleased with him, said: The Messenger of Allah, peace be upon him, said: **"Whoever guides others to goodness, he will be rewarded** (by Allah) **similarly to those who perform it."**

[Narrated by Muslim].

[20] – الحَدِيثُ العِشْرُون

عَنْ أَبِي هُرَيْـرَةَ، رَضِـيَ اللهُ عَنْهُ، قَالَ: قَالَ رَسُولُ اللهِ صلى الله عليه وسلم

((إِنَّ اللهَ تَعَالَى لَا يَنْظُرُ إِلَى أَجْسَامِكُمْ، وَلَا إِلَى صُوَرِكُمْ، وَلَكِنْ يَنْظُرُ إِلَى قُلُوبِكُمْ وَأَعْمَالِكُمْ))

رَوَاهُ مُسْلِم.

Abu Hurairah, may Allah be pleased with him, said: The Messenger of Allah, peace be upon him said:
"The Almighty Allah does not look at your bodies or your images, but He looks at your hearts and your deeds."
[Narrated by Muslim].

[21] - الحَدِيثُ الحَادِي وَالْعِشْرُون

عَنْ أَنَسِ بْنِ مَالِكٍ، رَضِـيَ اللهُ عَنْهُ، قَالَ: كَانَ أَكْثَرُ دُعَاءِ النَّبِيِّ صلى الله عليه وسلم:

((اللَّهُمَّ آتِنَا فِي الدُّنْيَا حَسَنَةً، وَفِي الآخِرَةِ حَسَنَةً، وَقِنَا عَذَابَ النَّارِ))

[رَوَاهُ البُخَارِي ومُسْلِم].

Anas, may Allah be pleased with him, said: The Prophet, Peace be upon him, often in his supplication was saying:
"O Allah, give us which is good in this world and the Hereafter, and protect us from the torment of the Fire."

[Narrated by Muslim].

الْقُرْآنُ الْكَرِيم

The Noble Qur'an

قَالَ اللهُ تَعَالَى:

﴿إِنَّ هَٰذَا ٱلْقُرْءَانَ يَهْدِى لِلَّتِى هِىَ أَقْوَمُ﴾

"Verily, this Qur'an guides to the Straight Path"

[الإسْرَاء: 9] [17: 9]

Qur'an Definition تَعْرِيفُ الْقُرْآن

الْقُرْآنُ الْكَرِيمُ: هُوَ كَلَامُ اللهِ - سُبْحَانَهُ وَتَعَالَى- الْمُنَزَّلُ عَلَى عَبْدِهِ وَرَسُولِهِ مُحَمَّدٍ، ﷺ، بِوَاسِطَةِ المَلَكِ جِبْرِيلَ عَلَيْهِ السَّلَام، المَنْقُولُ إِلَيْنَا بِالتَّوَاتر وَالْمَكْتُوبُ بَيْنَ دَفَّتَيِ المُصْحَفِ مِنْ أَوَّلِ سُورَةِ الْفَاتِحَةِ إِلَى آخِرِ سُورَةِ النَّاسِ، وَهُوَ الْمُعْجِزُ بِلَفْظِهِ ومَعْنَاه وَالْمُتَعَبَّدُ بِتِلَاوَتِهِ.

The Holy Qur'an is the words of Allah Almighty, revealed to His Servant and Messenger Muhammad, peace be upon him, by Angel Gabriel, peace be upon him. The Qur'an is transmitted to us complete and written as a textbook which started with the Opening Chapter (Surat Al-Fatihah) and ends with the Mankind Chapter (Surat An-Nas). The Qur'an is Miraculous in its phrases and its meaning and reciting it is worship.

The Revelation of the Qur'an – نُزُولُ الْقُرْآنِ الْكَرِيمِ

بَدَأَ نُزُولُ القُرْآنِ الكَرِيمِ عَلَى الرَّسُولِ مُحَمَّدٍ، ﷺ، فِي شَهْرِ رَمَضَانَ، فِي لَيْلَةِ القَدْرِ، عَلَى فَتَرَاتٍ مُتَقَطِّعَةٍ، وَاسْتَمَرَّ ذَلِكَ لِمُدَّةِ ثَلَاثٍ وَعِشْرِينَ سَنَةً. وَأَوَّلُ مَا نَزَلَ مِنَ الوَحْيِ: ﴿اقْرَأْ بِاسْمِ رَبِّكَ الَّذِي خَلَقَ * خَلَقَ الْإِنسَانَ مِنْ عَلَقٍ﴾ [العلق: 1-2].

The Holy Qur'an began to descend on the Prophet Muhammad, peace be upon him, during the month of Ramadan on the Night of the Power, the blessed Night.

The Qur'an was revealed at separate intervals over twenty-three years. The first verse revealed was: "Read in the name of your Lord Who created. He created man from a clot." [96: 1-2].

قَالَ تَعَالَى: ﴿شَهْرُ رَمَضَانَ الَّذِي أُنْزِلَ فِيهِ الْقُرْآنُ﴾ [البَقَرة: 185].

Allah said: "The month of Ramadan in which sent down the Qur'an." [2:185]

وَقَالَ تَعَالَى: ﴿إِنَّا أَنْزَلْنَاهُ فِي لَيْلَةِ الْقَدْرِ﴾ [القدر: 1].

Allah said: "Verily, We sent it (the Qur'an) down on the Night of Power." [97: 1].

وَقَالَ تَعَالَى: ﴿ إِنَّا أَنْزَلْنَاهُ فِي لَيْلَةٍ مُبَارَكَةٍ ﴾ [الدُّخان: 3].

Allah said: "Verily, We sent it down (the Qur'an) during a Blessed Night." [44: 3].

Names of the Qur'an – أَسْمَاءُ الْقُرْآنِ الْكَرِيمِ

لِلْقُرْآنِ الْكَرِيمِ أَسْمَاءٌ كَثِيرَةٌ مِنْهَا

The Holy Qur'an has many names, including:

1- الْقُرْآنُ الْعَظِيم - Al-Qur'an Al-Atheem (the Great)

قَالَ تَعَالَى: ﴿وَلَقَدْ آتَيْنَاكَ سَبْعًا مِّنَ الْمَثَانِي وَالْقُرْآنَ الْعَظِيمَ﴾ [الحِجْر: 87].

Allah said: "And indeed, We have certainly given you, seven of the Mathani (often repeated), and the great Qur'an" [15: 87].

2- الْقُرْآنُ الْحَكِيم - Al-Qur'an Al-Hakeem (The Wise)

قَالَ تَعَالَى: ﴿يسٓ ۝١ وَٱلْقُرْءَانِ ٱلْحَكِيمِ ۝٢﴾ [يسٓ: 1-2].

Allah said: **"**Ya, Seen. By the wise Qur'an.**"** [36: 1-2].

3- الْكِتَابُ - Al-Kitaab (The Book)

قَالَ تَعَالَى: ﴿حم وَالْكِتَابِ الْمُبِينِ﴾ [الدُّخان: 1-2]

Allah said: "Ha Meem. By the Book that makes things clear." [44: 1-2].

4- الْفُرْقَانُ - Al-Furqan (The Criterion)

قَالَ تَعَالَى: ﴿تَبَارَكَ الَّذِي نَزَّلَ الْفُرْقَانَ عَلَىٰ عَبْدِهِ﴾ [الفُرْقان: 1].

Allah said: **(**Blessed is He Who sent down the criterion to His slave." [25: 1].

5- النُّورُ - An-Noor (The Light)

قَالَ تَعَالَى: ﴿وَأَنزَلْنَا إِلَيْكُمْ نُورًا مُّبِينًا﴾ [النِّساء: 174]

Allah said: "And We have sent down unto you a manifest light." [4: 174].

6- التَّنْزِيلُ - At-Tanzeel (Revelation)

قَالَ تَعَالَى: ﴿وَإِنَّهُ لَتَنزِيلُ رَبِّ الْعَالَمِينَ﴾ [الشُّعَراء: 192].

Allah said: **"**Verily, this is a Revelation from the Lord of the Worlds." [26: 192].

Qur'an Virtues – فَضَائِلُ الْقُرْآنِ الْكَرِيمِ

Some of the Qur'an Virtues لِلْقُرْآنِ الْكَرِيمِ فَضَائِلُ كَثِيرَةٌ مِنْهَا:

1- الْهِدَايَةُ - Guidance

قَالَ اللهُ تَعَالَى: ﴿إِنَّ هَٰذَا ٱلْقُرْءَانَ يَهْدِى لِلَّتِى هِىَ أَقْوَمُ﴾ [الإسْراء: 9].

"Verily, this Qur'an guides to the Straight Path." [17: 9].

2- الشِّفَاءُ وَالرَّحْمَةُ - Healing and Mercy

قَالَ تَعَالَى: ﴿وَنُنَزِّلُ مِنَ الْقُرْآنِ مَا هُوَ شِفَاءٌ وَرَحْمَةٌ لِّلْمُؤْمِنِينَ﴾ [الإسْراء: 82].

"And We reveal of the Qur'an, that which is healing and mercy for the believers." [17: 82].

3- الشَّفَاعَةُ - Intercession

قَالَ رَسُولُ ﷺ: ((اِقْرَؤُوا الْقُرْآنَ فَإِنَّهُ يَأْتِي يَوْمَ الْقِيَامَةِ شَفِيعًا لِأَصْحَابِهِ)) [رَوَاهُ مُسْلِم].

"Read the Qur'an, because the Qur'an will come on the Day of Resurrection as an intercessor for its reciters." [Muslim].

4- الْخَيْرِيَّةُ - Blessing

قَالَ ﷺ: ((خَيْرُكُمْ مَنْ تَعَلَّمَ الْقُرْآنَ وَعَلَّمَهُ)) [رَوَاهُ البُخَارِي].

"The best among you is the one who learns the Qur'an and teaches it." [Narrated by Al-Bukhari].

5- الرِّفْعَةُ - Elevation (Superiority)

قَالَ ﷺ: ((إِنَّ اللهَ يَرْفَعُ بِهَذَا الْكِتَابِ أَقْوَامًا، وَيَضَعُ بِهِ آخَرِينَ)) [رَوَاهُ مُسْلِم].

"Verily, Allah by this book (Al-Qur'an) raises certain people, and He puts down others." [Muslim].

سُورَةُ الفَاتِحَةِ

بِسۡمِ ٱللَّهِ ٱلرَّحۡمَٰنِ ٱلرَّحِيمِ ١
ٱلۡحَمۡدُ لِلَّهِ رَبِّ ٱلۡعَٰلَمِينَ ٢ ٱلرَّحۡمَٰنِ ٱلرَّحِيمِ ٣
مَٰلِكِ يَوۡمِ ٱلدِّينِ ٤ إِيَّاكَ نَعۡبُدُ وَإِيَّاكَ نَسۡتَعِينُ ٥
ٱهۡدِنَا ٱلصِّرَٰطَ ٱلۡمُسۡتَقِيمَ ٦ صِرَٰطَ ٱلَّذِينَ أَنۡعَمۡتَ
عَلَيۡهِمۡ غَيۡرِ ٱلۡمَغۡضُوبِ عَلَيۡهِمۡ وَلَا ٱلضَّآلِّينَ ٧

In the Name of Allah, the Most Gracious, the Most Merciful (1)

All praise be to Allah the Lord of the worlds (2) The most Gracious, the Most Merciful (3) The Owner of the Day of Judgement (4) You (Alone) we worship, and You (Alone) we ask for help (5) Guide us to the Straight Path (Islam) (6) The Path of those on whom You have bestowed Your Grace, not (the way) of those who earned Your anger, nor of those who went astray (misguided) (7)

الفَاتِحَةُ: أَعْظَمُ سُورَةٍ فِي القُرْآنِ الكَرِيمِ وَقِرَاءَتُهَا أَحَدُ أَرْكَانِ الصَّلَاةِ، (تُقْرَأُ سُورَةُ الْفَاتِحَةِ فِي كُلِّ رَكْعَةٍ).

Al-Fatihah is the greatest Surah in the Holy Qur'an, and reading it is one of the pillars of prayer (Read Surat Al-Fatihah at every rak'ah).

آيَةُ الكُرسِي

﴿ ٱللَّهُ لَآ إِلَٰهَ إِلَّا هُوَ ٱلْحَىُّ ٱلْقَيُّومُ ۚ لَا تَأْخُذُهُۥ سِنَةٌ وَلَا نَوْمٌ ۚ لَّهُۥ مَا فِى ٱلسَّمَٰوَٰتِ وَمَا فِى ٱلْأَرْضِ ۗ مَن ذَا ٱلَّذِى يَشْفَعُ عِندَهُۥٓ إِلَّا بِإِذْنِهِۦ ۚ يَعْلَمُ مَا بَيْنَ أَيْدِيهِمْ وَمَا خَلْفَهُمْ ۖ وَلَا يُحِيطُونَ بِشَىْءٍ مِّنْ عِلْمِهِۦٓ إِلَّا بِمَا شَآءَ ۚ وَسِعَ كُرْسِيُّهُ ٱلسَّمَٰوَٰتِ وَٱلْأَرْضَ ۖ وَلَا يَـُٔودُهُۥ حِفْظُهُمَا ۚ وَهُوَ ٱلْعَلِىُّ ٱلْعَظِيمُ ﴾ [البقرة: 255].

"Allah! There is no deity except Him, the Ever-Living, the Sustainer of all that exists. Neither slumber (nap) can seize Him nor sleep. To Him belongs whatever is in the heavens, and whatever is on the earth. Who is he that can intercede with Him except by His permission? He knows what happens before them and what will happen after them. And they will not compass anything of His knowledge except for what He wills. His Kursi (a footstool or chair) extends over the heavens and the earth, and their preservation will not make Him tired. And He is the Most High, the Most Great." [2: 255].

آيَةُ الكُرْسِي: أَعْظَمُ آيَةٍ فِي القُرْآنِ الكَرِيمِ وَهِيَ حِصْنٌ مِنَ الشَّيْطَانِ لِمَنْ قَرَأَهَا قَبْلَ النَّوْمِ.

Ayat al-Kursi is the greatest verse in the Qur'an and is a fortress from the devil for those who read it before bed.

سُورَةُ القِيَامَةِ

بِسۡمِ ٱللَّهِ ٱلرَّحۡمَٰنِ ٱلرَّحِيمِ

لَآ أُقۡسِمُ بِيَوۡمِ ٱلۡقِيَٰمَةِ ﴿١﴾ وَلَآ أُقۡسِمُ بِٱلنَّفۡسِ ٱللَّوَّامَةِ ﴿٢﴾ أَيَحۡسَبُ
ٱلۡإِنسَٰنُ أَلَّن نَّجۡمَعَ عِظَامَهُۥ ﴿٣﴾ بَلَىٰ قَٰدِرِينَ عَلَىٰٓ أَن نُّسَوِّيَ بَنَانَهُۥ
﴿٤﴾ بَلۡ يُرِيدُ ٱلۡإِنسَٰنُ لِيَفۡجُرَ أَمَامَهُۥ ﴿٥﴾ يَسۡـَٔلُ أَيَّانَ يَوۡمُ ٱلۡقِيَٰمَةِ
﴿٦﴾ فَإِذَا بَرِقَ ٱلۡبَصَرُ ﴿٧﴾ وَخَسَفَ ٱلۡقَمَرُ ﴿٨﴾ وَجُمِعَ ٱلشَّمۡسُ وَٱلۡقَمَرُ
﴿٩﴾ يَقُولُ ٱلۡإِنسَٰنُ يَوۡمَئِذٍ أَيۡنَ ٱلۡمَفَرُّ ﴿١٠﴾ كَلَّا لَا وَزَرَ ﴿١١﴾ إِلَىٰ رَبِّكَ
يَوۡمَئِذٍ ٱلۡمُسۡتَقَرُّ ﴿١٢﴾ يُنَبَّؤُاْ ٱلۡإِنسَٰنُ يَوۡمَئِذِۭ بِمَا قَدَّمَ وَأَخَّرَ ﴿١٣﴾ بَلِ
ٱلۡإِنسَٰنُ عَلَىٰ نَفۡسِهِۦ بَصِيرَةٞ ﴿١٤﴾ وَلَوۡ أَلۡقَىٰ مَعَاذِيرَهُۥ ﴿١٥﴾ لَا تُحَرِّكۡ
بِهِۦ لِسَانَكَ لِتَعۡجَلَ بِهِۦٓ ﴿١٦﴾ إِنَّ عَلَيۡنَا جَمۡعَهُۥ وَقُرۡءَانَهُۥ ﴿١٧﴾ فَإِذَا
قَرَأۡنَٰهُ فَٱتَّبِعۡ قُرۡءَانَهُۥ ﴿١٨﴾ ثُمَّ إِنَّ عَلَيۡنَا بَيَانَهُۥ ﴿١٩﴾ كَلَّا بَلۡ تُحِبُّونَ
ٱلۡعَاجِلَةَ ﴿٢٠﴾ وَتَذَرُونَ ٱلۡأٓخِرَةَ ﴿٢١﴾ وُجُوهٞ يَوۡمَئِذٖ نَّاضِرَةٌ ﴿٢٢﴾ إِلَىٰ رَبِّهَا
نَاظِرَةٞ ﴿٢٣﴾ وَوُجُوهٞ يَوۡمَئِذِۭ بَاسِرَةٞ ﴿٢٤﴾ تَظُنُّ أَن يُفۡعَلَ بِهَا فَاقِرَةٞ ﴿٢٥﴾
كَلَّآ إِذَا بَلَغَتِ ٱلتَّرَاقِيَ ﴿٢٦﴾ وَقِيلَ مَنۡۜ رَاقٖ ﴿٢٧﴾ وَظَنَّ أَنَّهُ ٱلۡفِرَاقُ ﴿٢٨﴾
وَٱلۡتَفَّتِ ٱلسَّاقُ بِٱلسَّاقِ ﴿٢٩﴾ إِلَىٰ رَبِّكَ يَوۡمَئِذٍ ٱلۡمَسَاقُ ﴿٣٠﴾ فَلَا صَدَّقَ

وَلَا صَلَّىٰ ﴿٣١﴾ وَلَٰكِن كَذَّبَ وَتَوَلَّىٰ ﴿٣٢﴾ ثُمَّ ذَهَبَ إِلَىٰٓ أَهْلِهِۦ
يَتَمَطَّىٰٓ ﴿٣٣﴾ أَوْلَىٰ لَكَ فَأَوْلَىٰ ﴿٣٤﴾ ثُمَّ أَوْلَىٰ لَكَ فَأَوْلَىٰٓ ﴿٣٥﴾ أَيَحْسَبُ
ٱلْإِنسَٰنُ أَن يُتْرَكَ سُدًى ﴿٣٦﴾ أَلَمْ يَكُ نُطْفَةً مِّن مَّنِيٍّ يُمْنَىٰ ﴿٣٧﴾ ثُمَّ
كَانَ عَلَقَةً فَخَلَقَ فَسَوَّىٰ ﴿٣٨﴾ فَجَعَلَ مِنْهُ ٱلزَّوْجَيْنِ ٱلذَّكَرَ وَٱلْأُنثَىٰٓ
﴿٣٩﴾ أَلَيْسَ ذَٰلِكَ بِقَٰدِرٍ عَلَىٰٓ أَن يُحْـِۧىَ ٱلْمَوْتَىٰ ﴿٤٠﴾

سُورَةُ الإنْسَانِ

بِسْمِ ٱللَّهِ ٱلرَّحْمَٰنِ ٱلرَّحِيمِ
هَلْ أَتَىٰ عَلَى ٱلْإِنسَٰنِ حِينٌ مِّنَ ٱلدَّهْرِ لَمْ يَكُن شَيْـًٔا مَّذْكُورًا ﴿١﴾
إِنَّا خَلَقْنَا ٱلْإِنسَٰنَ مِن نُّطْفَةٍ أَمْشَاجٍ نَّبْتَلِيهِ فَجَعَلْنَٰهُ سَمِيعًۢا
بَصِيرًا ﴿٢﴾ إِنَّا هَدَيْنَٰهُ ٱلسَّبِيلَ إِمَّا شَاكِرًا وَإِمَّا كَفُورًا ﴿٣﴾ إِنَّآ
أَعْتَدْنَا لِلْكَٰفِرِينَ سَلَٰسِلَا۟ وَأَغْلَٰلًا وَسَعِيرًا ﴿٤﴾ إِنَّ ٱلْأَبْرَارَ
يَشْرَبُونَ مِن كَأْسٍ كَانَ مِزَاجُهَا كَافُورًا ﴿٥﴾ عَيْنًا يَشْرَبُ بِهَا عِبَادُ
ٱللَّهِ يُفَجِّرُونَهَا تَفْجِيرًا ﴿٦﴾ يُوفُونَ بِٱلنَّذْرِ وَيَخَافُونَ يَوْمًا كَانَ
شَرُّهُۥ مُسْتَطِيرًا ﴿٧﴾ وَيُطْعِمُونَ ٱلطَّعَامَ عَلَىٰ حُبِّهِۦ مِسْكِينًا وَيَتِيمًا
وَأَسِيرًا ﴿٨﴾ إِنَّمَا نُطْعِمُكُمْ لِوَجْهِ ٱللَّهِ لَا نُرِيدُ مِنكُمْ جَزَآءً وَلَا

شُكُورًا ﴿٩﴾ إِنَّا نَخَافُ مِن رَّبِّنَا يَوْمًا عَبُوسًا قَمْطَرِيرًا ﴿١٠﴾ فَوَقَاهُمُ
ٱللَّهُ شَرَّ ذَٰلِكَ ٱلْيَوْمِ وَلَقَّاهُمْ نَضْرَةً وَسُرُورًا ﴿١١﴾ وَجَزَاهُم بِمَا
صَبَرُوا۟ جَنَّةً وَحَرِيرًا ﴿١٢﴾ مُّتَّكِـِٔينَ فِيهَا عَلَى ٱلْأَرَآئِكِ ۖ لَا يَرَوْنَ
فِيهَا شَمْسًا وَلَا زَمْهَرِيرًا ﴿١٣﴾ وَدَانِيَةً عَلَيْهِمْ ظِلَالُهَا وَذُلِّلَتْ
قُطُوفُهَا تَذْلِيلًا ﴿١٤﴾ وَيُطَافُ عَلَيْهِم بِـَٔانِيَةٍ مِّن فِضَّةٍ وَأَكْوَابٍ
كَانَتْ قَوَارِيرَا۠ ﴿١٥﴾ قَوَارِيرَا۟ مِن فِضَّةٍ قَدَّرُوهَا تَقْدِيرًا ﴿١٦﴾ وَيُسْقَوْنَ
فِيهَا كَأْسًا كَانَ مِزَاجُهَا زَنجَبِيلًا ﴿١٧﴾ عَيْنًا فِيهَا تُسَمَّىٰ سَلْسَبِيلًا
﴿١٨﴾ ۞ وَيَطُوفُ عَلَيْهِمْ وِلْدَٰنٌ مُّخَلَّدُونَ إِذَا رَأَيْتَهُمْ حَسِبْتَهُمْ لُؤْلُؤًا
مَّنثُورًا ﴿١٩﴾ وَإِذَا رَأَيْتَ ثَمَّ رَأَيْتَ نَعِيمًا وَمُلْكًا كَبِيرًا ﴿٢٠﴾ عَٰلِيَهُمْ
ثِيَابُ سُندُسٍ خُضْرٌ وَإِسْتَبْرَقٌ ۖ وَحُلُّوٓا۟ أَسَاوِرَ مِن فِضَّةٍ وَسَقَاهُمْ
رَبُّهُمْ شَرَابًا طَهُورًا ﴿٢١﴾ إِنَّ هَٰذَا كَانَ لَكُمْ جَزَآءً وَكَانَ سَعْيُكُم
مَّشْكُورًا ﴿٢٢﴾ إِنَّا نَحْنُ نَزَّلْنَا عَلَيْكَ ٱلْقُرْءَانَ تَنزِيلًا ﴿٢٣﴾ فَٱصْبِرْ
لِحُكْمِ رَبِّكَ وَلَا تُطِعْ مِنْهُمْ ءَاثِمًا أَوْ كَفُورًا ﴿٢٤﴾ وَٱذْكُرِ ٱسْمَ
رَبِّكَ بُكْرَةً وَأَصِيلًا ﴿٢٥﴾ وَمِنَ ٱلَّيْلِ فَٱسْجُدْ لَهُۥ وَسَبِّحْهُ لَيْلًا
طَوِيلًا ﴿٢٦﴾ إِنَّ هَٰٓؤُلَآءِ يُحِبُّونَ ٱلْعَاجِلَةَ وَيَذَرُونَ وَرَآءَهُمْ يَوْمًا ثَقِيلًا

﴿٢٧﴾ نَّحۡنُ خَلَقۡنَٰهُمۡ وَشَدَدۡنَآ أَسۡرَهُمۡۖ وَإِذَا شِئۡنَا بَدَّلۡنَآ أَمۡثَٰلَهُمۡ
تَبۡدِيلًا ﴿٢٨﴾ إِنَّ هَٰذِهِۦ تَذۡكِرَةٞۖ فَمَن شَآءَ ٱتَّخَذَ إِلَىٰ رَبِّهِۦ سَبِيلٗا ﴿٢٩﴾
وَمَا تَشَآءُونَ إِلَّآ أَن يَشَآءَ ٱللَّهُۚ إِنَّ ٱللَّهَ كَانَ عَلِيمًا حَكِيمٗا ﴿٣٠﴾
يُدۡخِلُ مَن يَشَآءُ فِي رَحۡمَتِهِۦۚ وَٱلظَّٰلِمِينَ أَعَدَّ لَهُمۡ عَذَابًا أَلِيمَۢا ﴿٣١﴾

سُورَةُ المُرْسَلاتِ

بِسۡمِ ٱللَّهِ ٱلرَّحۡمَٰنِ ٱلرَّحِيمِ

وَٱلۡمُرۡسَلَٰتِ عُرۡفٗا ﴿١﴾ فَٱلۡعَٰصِفَٰتِ عَصۡفٗا ﴿٢﴾ وَٱلنَّٰشِرَٰتِ نَشۡرٗا ﴿٣﴾
فَٱلۡفَٰرِقَٰتِ فَرۡقٗا ﴿٤﴾ فَٱلۡمُلۡقِيَٰتِ ذِكۡرًا ﴿٥﴾ عُذۡرًا أَوۡ نُذۡرًا ﴿٦﴾ إِنَّمَا
تُوعَدُونَ لَوَٰقِعٞ ﴿٧﴾ فَإِذَا ٱلنُّجُومُ طُمِسَتۡ ﴿٨﴾ وَإِذَا ٱلسَّمَآءُ فُرِجَتۡ
﴿٩﴾ وَإِذَا ٱلۡجِبَالُ نُسِفَتۡ ﴿١٠﴾ وَإِذَا ٱلرُّسُلُ أُقِّتَتۡ ﴿١١﴾ لِأَيِّ يَوۡمٍ أُجِّلَتۡ
﴿١٢﴾ لِيَوۡمِ ٱلۡفَصۡلِ ﴿١٣﴾ وَمَآ أَدۡرَىٰكَ مَا يَوۡمُ ٱلۡفَصۡلِ ﴿١٤﴾ وَيۡلٞ يَوۡمَئِذٖ
لِّلۡمُكَذِّبِينَ ﴿١٥﴾ أَلَمۡ نُهۡلِكِ ٱلۡأَوَّلِينَ ﴿١٦﴾ ثُمَّ نُتۡبِعُهُمُ ٱلۡأٓخِرِينَ ﴿١٧﴾
كَذَٰلِكَ نَفۡعَلُ بِٱلۡمُجۡرِمِينَ ﴿١٨﴾ وَيۡلٞ يَوۡمَئِذٖ لِّلۡمُكَذِّبِينَ ﴿١٩﴾ أَلَمۡ
نَخۡلُقكُّم مِّن مَّآءٖ مَّهِينٖ ﴿٢٠﴾ فَجَعَلۡنَٰهُ فِي قَرَارٖ مَّكِينٍ ﴿٢١﴾ إِلَىٰ قَدَرٖ
مَّعۡلُومٖ ﴿٢٢﴾ فَقَدَرۡنَا فَنِعۡمَ ٱلۡقَٰدِرُونَ ﴿٢٣﴾ وَيۡلٞ يَوۡمَئِذٖ لِّلۡمُكَذِّبِينَ ﴿٢٤﴾

أَلَمْ نَجْعَلِ ٱلْأَرْضَ كِفَاتًا ﴿٢٥﴾ أَحْيَآءً وَأَمْوَٰتًا ﴿٢٦﴾ وَجَعَلْنَا فِيهَا
رَوَٰسِىَ شَٰمِخَٰتٍ وَأَسْقَيْنَٰكُم مَّآءً فُرَاتًا ﴿٢٧﴾ وَيْلٌ يَوْمَئِذٍ
لِّلْمُكَذِّبِينَ ﴿٢٨﴾ ٱنطَلِقُوٓا۟ إِلَىٰ مَا كُنتُم بِهِۦ تُكَذِّبُونَ ﴿٢٩﴾ ٱنطَلِقُوٓا۟
إِلَىٰ ظِلٍّ ذِى ثَلَٰثِ شُعَبٍ ﴿٣٠﴾ لَّا ظَلِيلٍ وَلَا يُغْنِى مِنَ ٱللَّهَبِ ﴿٣١﴾
إِنَّهَا تَرْمِى بِشَرَرٍ كَٱلْقَصْرِ ﴿٣٢﴾ كَأَنَّهُۥ جِمَٰلَتٌ صُفْرٌ ﴿٣٣﴾ وَيْلٌ
يَوْمَئِذٍ لِّلْمُكَذِّبِينَ ﴿٣٤﴾ هَٰذَا يَوْمُ لَا يَنطِقُونَ ﴿٣٥﴾ وَلَا يُؤْذَنُ لَهُمْ
فَيَعْتَذِرُونَ ﴿٣٦﴾ وَيْلٌ يَوْمَئِذٍ لِّلْمُكَذِّبِينَ ﴿٣٧﴾ هَٰذَا يَوْمُ ٱلْفَصْلِ ۖ
جَمَعْنَٰكُمْ وَٱلْأَوَّلِينَ ﴿٣٨﴾ فَإِن كَانَ لَكُمْ كَيْدٌ فَكِيدُونِ ﴿٣٩﴾ وَيْلٌ
يَوْمَئِذٍ لِّلْمُكَذِّبِينَ ﴿٤٠﴾ إِنَّ ٱلْمُتَّقِينَ فِى ظِلَٰلٍ وَعُيُونٍ ﴿٤١﴾ وَفَوَٰكِهَ
مِمَّا يَشْتَهُونَ ﴿٤٢﴾ كُلُوا۟ وَٱشْرَبُوا۟ هَنِيٓـًٔا بِمَا كُنتُمْ تَعْمَلُونَ ﴿٤٣﴾ إِنَّا
كَذَٰلِكَ نَجْزِى ٱلْمُحْسِنِينَ ﴿٤٤﴾ وَيْلٌ يَوْمَئِذٍ لِّلْمُكَذِّبِينَ ﴿٤٥﴾ كُلُوا۟
وَتَمَتَّعُوا۟ قَلِيلًا إِنَّكُم مُّجْرِمُونَ ﴿٤٦﴾ وَيْلٌ يَوْمَئِذٍ لِّلْمُكَذِّبِينَ ﴿٤٧﴾
وَإِذَا قِيلَ لَهُمُ ٱرْكَعُوا۟ لَا يَرْكَعُونَ ﴿٤٨﴾ وَيْلٌ يَوْمَئِذٍ لِّلْمُكَذِّبِينَ ﴿٤٩﴾
فَبِأَىِّ حَدِيثٍۭ بَعْدَهُۥ يُؤْمِنُونَ ﴿٥٠﴾

سُورَةُ النَّبَإِ

بِسْمِ ٱللَّهِ ٱلرَّحْمَٰنِ ٱلرَّحِيمِ

عَمَّ يَتَسَآءَلُونَ ١ عَنِ ٱلنَّبَإِ ٱلْعَظِيمِ ٢ ٱلَّذِى هُمْ فِيهِ مُخْتَلِفُونَ
٣ كَلَّا سَيَعْلَمُونَ ٤ ثُمَّ كَلَّا سَيَعْلَمُونَ ٥ أَلَمْ نَجْعَلِ ٱلْأَرْضَ
مِهَٰدًا ٦ وَٱلْجِبَالَ أَوْتَادًا ٧ وَخَلَقْنَٰكُمْ أَزْوَٰجًا ٨ وَجَعَلْنَا
نَوْمَكُمْ سُبَاتًا ٩ وَجَعَلْنَا ٱلَّيْلَ لِبَاسًا ١٠ وَجَعَلْنَا ٱلنَّهَارَ مَعَاشًا
١١ وَبَنَيْنَا فَوْقَكُمْ سَبْعًا شِدَادًا ١٢ وَجَعَلْنَا سِرَاجًا وَهَّاجًا ١٣
وَأَنزَلْنَا مِنَ ٱلْمُعْصِرَٰتِ مَآءً ثَجَّاجًا ١٤ لِّنُخْرِجَ بِهِۦ حَبًّا وَنَبَاتًا ١٥
وَجَنَّٰتٍ أَلْفَافًا ١٦ إِنَّ يَوْمَ ٱلْفَصْلِ كَانَ مِيقَٰتًا ١٧ يَوْمَ يُنفَخُ فِى
ٱلصُّورِ فَتَأْتُونَ أَفْوَاجًا ١٨ وَفُتِحَتِ ٱلسَّمَآءُ فَكَانَتْ أَبْوَٰبًا ١٩
وَسُيِّرَتِ ٱلْجِبَالُ فَكَانَتْ سَرَابًا ٢٠ إِنَّ جَهَنَّمَ كَانَتْ مِرْصَادًا ٢١
لِّلطَّٰغِينَ مَـَٔابًا ٢٢ لَّٰبِثِينَ فِيهَآ أَحْقَابًا ٢٣ لَّا يَذُوقُونَ فِيهَا بَرْدًا
وَلَا شَرَابًا ٢٤ إِلَّا حَمِيمًا وَغَسَّاقًا ٢٥ جَزَآءً وِفَاقًا ٢٦ إِنَّهُمْ كَانُوا۟ لَا
يَرْجُونَ حِسَابًا ٢٧ وَكَذَّبُوا۟ بِـَٔايَٰتِنَا كِذَّابًا ٢٨ وَكُلَّ شَىْءٍ أَحْصَيْنَٰهُ
كِتَٰبًا ٢٩ فَذُوقُوا۟ فَلَن نَّزِيدَكُمْ إِلَّا عَذَابًا ٣٠ إِنَّ لِلْمُتَّقِينَ مَفَازًا
٣١ حَدَآئِقَ وَأَعْنَٰبًا ٣٢ وَكَوَاعِبَ أَتْرَابًا ٣٣ وَكَأْسًا دِهَاقًا ٣٤ لَّا
يَسْمَعُونَ فِيهَا لَغْوًا وَلَا كِذَّٰبًا ٣٥ جَزَآءً مِّن رَّبِّكَ عَطَآءً

حِسَابًا ﴿٣٦﴾ رَّبِّ ٱلسَّمَٰوَٰتِ وَٱلۡأَرۡضِ وَمَا بَيۡنَهُمَا ٱلرَّحۡمَٰنِۖ لَا
يَمۡلِكُونَ مِنۡهُ خِطَابًا ﴿٣٧﴾ يَوۡمَ يَقُومُ ٱلرُّوحُ وَٱلۡمَلَٰٓئِكَةُ صَفًّاۖ لَّا
يَتَكَلَّمُونَ إِلَّا مَنۡ أَذِنَ لَهُ ٱلرَّحۡمَٰنُ وَقَالَ صَوَابًا ﴿٣٨﴾ ذَٰلِكَ ٱلۡيَوۡمُ
ٱلۡحَقُّۖ فَمَن شَآءَ ٱتَّخَذَ إِلَىٰ رَبِّهِۦ مَـَٔابًا ﴿٣٩﴾ إِنَّآ أَنذَرۡنَٰكُمۡ عَذَابًا
قَرِيبًا يَوۡمَ يَنظُرُ ٱلۡمَرۡءُ مَا قَدَّمَتۡ يَدَاهُ وَيَقُولُ ٱلۡكَافِرُ يَٰلَيۡتَنِي
كُنتُ تُرَٰبَۢا ﴿٤٠﴾

سُورَةُ النَّزِعَاتِ

بِسۡمِ ٱللَّهِ ٱلرَّحۡمَٰنِ ٱلرَّحِيمِ

وَٱلنَّٰزِعَٰتِ غَرۡقًا ﴿١﴾ وَٱلنَّٰشِطَٰتِ نَشۡطًا ﴿٢﴾ وَٱلسَّٰبِحَٰتِ سَبۡحًا ﴿٣﴾
فَٱلسَّٰبِقَٰتِ سَبۡقًا ﴿٤﴾ فَٱلۡمُدَبِّرَٰتِ أَمۡرًا ﴿٥﴾ يَوۡمَ تَرۡجُفُ ٱلرَّاجِفَةُ ﴿٦﴾
تَتۡبَعُهَا ٱلرَّادِفَةُ ﴿٧﴾ قُلُوبٌ يَوۡمَئِذٍ وَاجِفَةٌ ﴿٨﴾ أَبۡصَٰرُهَا خَٰشِعَةٌ ﴿٩﴾
يَقُولُونَ أَءِنَّا لَمَرۡدُودُونَ فِي ٱلۡحَافِرَةِ ﴿١٠﴾ أَءِذَا كُنَّا عِظَٰمًا نَّخِرَةً ﴿١١﴾
قَالُواْ تِلۡكَ إِذًا كَرَّةٌ خَاسِرَةٌ ﴿١٢﴾ فَإِنَّمَا هِيَ زَجۡرَةٌ وَٰحِدَةٌ ﴿١٣﴾ فَإِذَا هُم
بِٱلسَّاهِرَةِ ﴿١٤﴾ هَلۡ أَتَىٰكَ حَدِيثُ مُوسَىٰٓ ﴿١٥﴾ إِذۡ نَادَىٰهُ رَبُّهُۥ بِٱلۡوَادِ
ٱلۡمُقَدَّسِ طُوًى ﴿١٦﴾ ٱذۡهَبۡ إِلَىٰ فِرۡعَوۡنَ إِنَّهُۥ طَغَىٰ ﴿١٧﴾ فَقُلۡ هَل لَّكَ
إِلَىٰٓ أَن تَزَكَّىٰ ﴿١٨﴾ وَأَهۡدِيَكَ إِلَىٰ رَبِّكَ فَتَخۡشَىٰ ﴿١٩﴾ فَأَرَىٰهُ ٱلۡأٓيَةَ
ٱلۡكُبۡرَىٰ ﴿٢٠﴾ فَكَذَّبَ وَعَصَىٰ ﴿٢١﴾ ثُمَّ أَدۡبَرَ يَسۡعَىٰ ﴿٢٢﴾ فَحَشَرَ فَنَادَىٰ

﴿٢٣﴾ فَقَالَ أَنَا۠ رَبُّكُمُ ٱلۡأَعۡلَىٰ ﴿٢٤﴾ فَأَخَذَهُ ٱللَّهُ نَكَالَ ٱلۡأٓخِرَةِ
وَٱلۡأُولَىٰٓ ﴿٢٥﴾ إِنَّ فِي ذَٰلِكَ لَعِبۡرَةٗ لِّمَن يَخۡشَىٰٓ ﴿٢٦﴾ ءَأَنتُمۡ أَشَدُّ خَلۡقًا أَمِ
ٱلسَّمَآءُۚ بَنَىٰهَا ﴿٢٧﴾ رَفَعَ سَمۡكَهَا فَسَوَّىٰهَا ﴿٢٨﴾ وَأَغۡطَشَ لَيۡلَهَا وَأَخۡرَجَ
ضُحَىٰهَا ﴿٢٩﴾ وَٱلۡأَرۡضَ بَعۡدَ ذَٰلِكَ دَحَىٰهَآ ﴿٣٠﴾ أَخۡرَجَ مِنۡهَا مَآءَهَا
وَمَرۡعَىٰهَا ﴿٣١﴾ وَٱلۡجِبَالَ أَرۡسَىٰهَا ﴿٣٢﴾ مَتَٰعٗا لَّكُمۡ وَلِأَنۡعَٰمِكُمۡ ﴿٣٣﴾
فَإِذَا جَآءَتِ ٱلطَّآمَّةُ ٱلۡكُبۡرَىٰ ﴿٣٤﴾ يَوۡمَ يَتَذَكَّرُ ٱلۡإِنسَٰنُ مَا سَعَىٰ ﴿٣٥﴾
وَبُرِّزَتِ ٱلۡجَحِيمُ لِمَن يَرَىٰ ﴿٣٦﴾ فَأَمَّا مَن طَغَىٰ ﴿٣٧﴾ وَءَاثَرَ ٱلۡحَيَوٰةَ
ٱلدُّنۡيَا ﴿٣٨﴾ فَإِنَّ ٱلۡجَحِيمَ هِيَ ٱلۡمَأۡوَىٰ ﴿٣٩﴾ وَأَمَّا مَنۡ خَافَ مَقَامَ رَبِّهِۦ
وَنَهَى ٱلنَّفۡسَ عَنِ ٱلۡهَوَىٰ ﴿٤٠﴾ فَإِنَّ ٱلۡجَنَّةَ هِيَ ٱلۡمَأۡوَىٰ ﴿٤١﴾ يَسۡـَٔلُونَكَ
عَنِ ٱلسَّاعَةِ أَيَّانَ مُرۡسَىٰهَا ﴿٤٢﴾ فِيمَ أَنتَ مِن ذِكۡرَىٰهَآ ﴿٤٣﴾ إِلَىٰ رَبِّكَ
مُنتَهَىٰهَآ ﴿٤٤﴾ إِنَّمَآ أَنتَ مُنذِرُ مَن يَخۡشَىٰهَا ﴿٤٥﴾ كَأَنَّهُمۡ يَوۡمَ يَرَوۡنَهَا
لَمۡ يَلۡبَثُوٓاْ إِلَّا عَشِيَّةً أَوۡ ضُحَىٰهَا ﴿٤٦﴾

سُورَةُ عَبَسَ

بِسۡمِ ٱللَّهِ ٱلرَّحۡمَٰنِ ٱلرَّحِيمِ

عَبَسَ وَتَوَلَّىٰٓ ﴿١﴾ أَن جَآءَهُ ٱلۡأَعۡمَىٰ ﴿٢﴾ وَمَا يُدۡرِيكَ لَعَلَّهُۥ يَزَّكَّىٰٓ ﴿٣﴾
أَوۡ يَذَّكَّرُ فَتَنفَعَهُ ٱلذِّكۡرَىٰٓ ﴿٤﴾ أَمَّا مَنِ ٱسۡتَغۡنَىٰ ﴿٥﴾ فَأَنتَ لَهُۥ تَصَدَّىٰ
﴿٦﴾ وَمَا عَلَيۡكَ أَلَّا يَزَّكَّىٰ ﴿٧﴾ وَأَمَّا مَن جَآءَكَ يَسۡعَىٰ ﴿٨﴾ وَهُوَ يَخۡشَىٰ

٩ فَأَنتَ عَنۡهُ تَلَهَّىٰ ١٠ كَلَّآ إِنَّهَا تَذۡكِرَةٞ ١١ فَمَن شَآءَ ذَكَرَهُۥ ١٢
فِي صُحُفٖ مُّكَرَّمَةٖ ١٣ مَّرۡفُوعَةٖ مُّطَهَّرَةِۭ ١٤ بِأَيۡدِي سَفَرَةٖ ١٥ كِرَامِۭ
بَرَرَةٖ ١٦ قُتِلَ ٱلۡإِنسَٰنُ مَآ أَكۡفَرَهُۥ ١٧ مِنۡ أَيِّ شَيۡءٍ خَلَقَهُۥ ١٨
مِن نُّطۡفَةٍ خَلَقَهُۥ فَقَدَّرَهُۥ ١٩ ثُمَّ ٱلسَّبِيلَ يَسَّرَهُۥ ٢٠ ثُمَّ أَمَاتَهُۥ
فَأَقۡبَرَهُۥ ٢١ ثُمَّ إِذَا شَآءَ أَنشَرَهُۥ ٢٢ كَلَّا لَمَّا يَقۡضِ مَآ أَمَرَهُۥ ٢٣
فَلۡيَنظُرِ ٱلۡإِنسَٰنُ إِلَىٰ طَعَامِهِۦٓ ٢٤ أَنَّا صَبَبۡنَا ٱلۡمَآءَ صَبّٗا ٢٥ ثُمَّ شَقَقۡنَا
ٱلۡأَرۡضَ شَقّٗا ٢٦ فَأَنۢبَتۡنَا فِيهَا حَبّٗا ٢٧ وَعِنَبٗا وَقَضۡبٗا ٢٨ وَزَيۡتُونٗا
وَنَخۡلٗا ٢٩ وَحَدَآئِقَ غُلۡبٗا ٣٠ وَفَٰكِهَةٗ وَأَبّٗا ٣١ مَّتَٰعٗا لَّكُمۡ
وَلِأَنۡعَٰمِكُمۡ ٣٢ فَإِذَا جَآءَتِ ٱلصَّآخَّةُ ٣٣ يَوۡمَ يَفِرُّ ٱلۡمَرۡءُ مِنۡ أَخِيهِ
٣٤ وَأُمِّهِۦ وَأَبِيهِ ٣٥ وَصَٰحِبَتِهِۦ وَبَنِيهِ ٣٦ لِكُلِّ ٱمۡرِيٕٖ مِّنۡهُمۡ يَوۡمَئِذٖ
شَأۡنٞ يُغۡنِيهِ ٣٧ وُجُوهٞ يَوۡمَئِذٖ مُّسۡفِرَةٞ ٣٨ ضَاحِكَةٞ مُّسۡتَبۡشِرَةٞ ٣٩
وَوُجُوهٞ يَوۡمَئِذٍ عَلَيۡهَا غَبَرَةٞ ٤٠ تَرۡهَقُهَا قَتَرَةٌ ٤١ أُوْلَٰٓئِكَ هُمُ ٱلۡكَفَرَةُ
ٱلۡفَجَرَةُ ٤٢

سُورَةُ التَّكۡوِيرِ

بِسۡمِ ٱللَّهِ ٱلرَّحۡمَٰنِ ٱلرَّحِيمِ

إِذَا ٱلشَّمۡسُ كُوِّرَتۡ ١ وَإِذَا ٱلنُّجُومُ ٱنكَدَرَتۡ ٢ وَإِذَا ٱلۡجِبَالُ
سُيِّرَتۡ ٣ وَإِذَا ٱلۡعِشَارُ عُطِّلَتۡ ٤ وَإِذَا ٱلۡوُحُوشُ حُشِرَتۡ ٥

وَإِذَا ٱلْبِحَارُ سُجِّرَتْ ﴿٦﴾ وَإِذَا ٱلنُّفُوسُ زُوِّجَتْ ﴿٧﴾ وَإِذَا ٱلْمَوْءُۥدَةُ
سُئِلَتْ ﴿٨﴾ بِأَىِّ ذَنۢبٍ قُتِلَتْ ﴿٩﴾ وَإِذَا ٱلصُّحُفُ نُشِرَتْ ﴿١٠﴾ وَإِذَا
ٱلسَّمَآءُ كُشِطَتْ ﴿١١﴾ وَإِذَا ٱلْجَحِيمُ سُعِّرَتْ ﴿١٢﴾ وَإِذَا ٱلْجَنَّةُ أُزْلِفَتْ
﴿١٣﴾ عَلِمَتْ نَفْسٌ مَّآ أَحْضَرَتْ ﴿١٤﴾ فَلَآ أُقْسِمُ بِٱلْخُنَّسِ ﴿١٥﴾ ٱلْجَوَارِ
ٱلْكُنَّسِ ﴿١٦﴾ وَٱلَّيْلِ إِذَا عَسْعَسَ ﴿١٧﴾ وَٱلصُّبْحِ إِذَا تَنَفَّسَ ﴿١٨﴾ إِنَّهُۥ
لَقَوْلُ رَسُولٍ كَرِيمٍ ﴿١٩﴾ ذِى قُوَّةٍ عِندَ ذِى ٱلْعَرْشِ مَكِينٍ ﴿٢٠﴾ مُّطَاعٍ
ثَمَّ أَمِينٍ ﴿٢١﴾ وَمَا صَاحِبُكُم بِمَجْنُونٍ ﴿٢٢﴾ وَلَقَدْ رَءَاهُ بِٱلْأُفُقِ
ٱلْمُبِينِ ﴿٢٣﴾ وَمَا هُوَ عَلَى ٱلْغَيْبِ بِضَنِينٍ ﴿٢٤﴾ وَمَا هُوَ بِقَوْلِ شَيْطَٰنٍ
رَّجِيمٍ ﴿٢٥﴾ فَأَيْنَ تَذْهَبُونَ ﴿٢٦﴾ إِنْ هُوَ إِلَّا ذِكْرٌ لِّلْعَٰلَمِينَ ﴿٢٧﴾ لِمَن
شَآءَ مِنكُمْ أَن يَسْتَقِيمَ ﴿٢٨﴾ وَمَا تَشَآءُونَ إِلَّآ أَن يَشَآءَ ٱللَّهُ رَبُّ
ٱلْعَٰلَمِينَ ﴿٢٩﴾

سُورَةُ الإنفِطَارِ

بِسْمِ ٱللَّهِ ٱلرَّحْمَٰنِ ٱلرَّحِيمِ

إِذَا ٱلسَّمَآءُ ٱنفَطَرَتْ ﴿١﴾ وَإِذَا ٱلْكَوَاكِبُ ٱنتَثَرَتْ ﴿٢﴾ وَإِذَا ٱلْبِحَارُ
فُجِّرَتْ ﴿٣﴾ وَإِذَا ٱلْقُبُورُ بُعْثِرَتْ ﴿٤﴾ عَلِمَتْ نَفْسٌ مَّا قَدَّمَتْ
وَأَخَّرَتْ ﴿٥﴾ يَٰٓأَيُّهَا ٱلْإِنسَٰنُ مَا غَرَّكَ بِرَبِّكَ ٱلْكَرِيمِ ﴿٦﴾ ٱلَّذِى
خَلَقَكَ فَسَوَّىٰكَ فَعَدَلَكَ ﴿٧﴾ فِىٓ أَىِّ صُورَةٍ مَّا شَآءَ رَكَّبَكَ ﴿٨﴾ كَلَّا

بَلْ تُكَذِّبُونَ بِٱلدِّينِ ﴿٩﴾ وَإِنَّ عَلَيْكُمْ لَحَـٰفِظِينَ ﴿١٠﴾ كِرَامًا
كَـٰتِبِينَ ﴿١١﴾ يَعْلَمُونَ مَا تَفْعَلُونَ ﴿١٢﴾ إِنَّ ٱلْأَبْرَارَ لَفِى نَعِيمٍ ﴿١٣﴾
وَإِنَّ ٱلْفُجَّارَ لَفِى جَحِيمٍ ﴿١٤﴾ يَصْلَوْنَهَا يَوْمَ ٱلدِّينِ ﴿١٥﴾ وَمَا هُمْ عَنْهَا
بِغَآئِبِينَ ﴿١٦﴾ وَمَآ أَدْرَىٰكَ مَا يَوْمُ ٱلدِّينِ ﴿١٧﴾ ثُمَّ مَآ أَدْرَىٰكَ مَا يَوْمُ
ٱلدِّينِ ﴿١٨﴾ يَوْمَ لَا تَمْلِكُ نَفْسٌ لِّنَفْسٍ شَيْـًٔا ۖ وَٱلْأَمْرُ يَوْمَئِذٍ لِّلَّهِ ﴿١٩﴾

سُورَةُ المُطَفِّفِين

بِسْمِ ٱللَّهِ ٱلرَّحْمَـٰنِ ٱلرَّحِيمِ

وَيْلٌ لِّلْمُطَفِّفِينَ ﴿١﴾ ٱلَّذِينَ إِذَا ٱكْتَالُوا۟ عَلَى ٱلنَّاسِ يَسْتَوْفُونَ ﴿٢﴾
وَإِذَا كَالُوهُمْ أَو وَّزَنُوهُمْ يُخْسِرُونَ ﴿٣﴾ أَلَا يَظُنُّ أُو۟لَـٰٓئِكَ أَنَّهُم
مَّبْعُوثُونَ ﴿٤﴾ لِيَوْمٍ عَظِيمٍ ﴿٥﴾ يَوْمَ يَقُومُ ٱلنَّاسُ لِرَبِّ ٱلْعَـٰلَمِينَ ﴿٦﴾
كَلَّآ إِنَّ كِتَـٰبَ ٱلْفُجَّارِ لَفِى سِجِّينٍ ﴿٧﴾ وَمَآ أَدْرَىٰكَ مَا سِجِّينٌ ﴿٨﴾
كِتَـٰبٌ مَّرْقُومٌ ﴿٩﴾ وَيْلٌ يَوْمَئِذٍ لِّلْمُكَذِّبِينَ ﴿١٠﴾ ٱلَّذِينَ يُكَذِّبُونَ بِيَوْمِ
ٱلدِّينِ ﴿١١﴾ وَمَا يُكَذِّبُ بِهِۦٓ إِلَّا كُلُّ مُعْتَدٍ أَثِيمٍ ﴿١٢﴾ إِذَا تُتْلَىٰ عَلَيْهِ
ءَايَـٰتُنَا قَالَ أَسَـٰطِيرُ ٱلْأَوَّلِينَ ﴿١٣﴾ كَلَّا ۖ بَلْ ۜ رَانَ عَلَىٰ قُلُوبِهِم مَّا كَانُوا۟
يَكْسِبُونَ ﴿١٤﴾ كَلَّآ إِنَّهُمْ عَن رَّبِّهِمْ يَوْمَئِذٍ لَّمَحْجُوبُونَ ﴿١٥﴾ ثُمَّ إِنَّهُمْ
لَصَالُوا۟ ٱلْجَحِيمِ ﴿١٦﴾ ثُمَّ يُقَالُ هَـٰذَا ٱلَّذِى كُنتُم بِهِۦ تُكَذِّبُونَ ﴿١٧﴾

كَلَّآ إِنَّ كِتَٰبَ ٱلْأَبْرَارِ لَفِى عِلِّيِّينَ ﴿١٨﴾ وَمَآ أَدْرَىٰكَ مَا عِلِّيُّونَ ﴿١٩﴾
كِتَٰبٌ مَّرْقُومٌ ﴿٢٠﴾ يَشْهَدُهُ ٱلْمُقَرَّبُونَ ﴿٢١﴾ إِنَّ ٱلْأَبْرَارَ لَفِى نَعِيمٍ ﴿٢٢﴾
عَلَى ٱلْأَرَآئِكِ يَنظُرُونَ ﴿٢٣﴾ تَعْرِفُ فِى وُجُوهِهِمْ نَضْرَةَ ٱلنَّعِيمِ ﴿٢٤﴾
يُسْقَوْنَ مِن رَّحِيقٍ مَّخْتُومٍ ﴿٢٥﴾ خِتَٰمُهُۥ مِسْكٌ ۚ وَفِى ذَٰلِكَ فَلْيَتَنَافَسِ
ٱلْمُتَنَٰفِسُونَ ﴿٢٦﴾ وَمِزَاجُهُۥ مِن تَسْنِيمٍ ﴿٢٧﴾ عَيْنًا يَشْرَبُ بِهَا
ٱلْمُقَرَّبُونَ ﴿٢٨﴾ إِنَّ ٱلَّذِينَ أَجْرَمُوا۟ كَانُوا۟ مِنَ ٱلَّذِينَ ءَامَنُوا۟ يَضْحَكُونَ
﴿٢٩﴾ وَإِذَا مَرُّوا۟ بِهِمْ يَتَغَامَزُونَ ﴿٣٠﴾ وَإِذَا ٱنقَلَبُوٓا۟ إِلَىٰٓ أَهْلِهِمُ ٱنقَلَبُوا۟
فَكِهِينَ ﴿٣١﴾ وَإِذَا رَأَوْهُمْ قَالُوٓا۟ إِنَّ هَٰٓؤُلَآءِ لَضَآلُّونَ ﴿٣٢﴾ وَمَآ أُرْسِلُوا۟
عَلَيْهِمْ حَٰفِظِينَ ﴿٣٣﴾ فَٱلْيَوْمَ ٱلَّذِينَ ءَامَنُوا۟ مِنَ ٱلْكُفَّارِ يَضْحَكُونَ
﴿٣٤﴾ عَلَى ٱلْأَرَآئِكِ يَنظُرُونَ ﴿٣٥﴾ هَلْ ثُوِّبَ ٱلْكُفَّارُ مَا كَانُوا۟ يَفْعَلُونَ ﴿٣٦﴾

سُورَةُ الإنْشِقَاق

بِسْمِ ٱللَّهِ ٱلرَّحْمَٰنِ ٱلرَّحِيمِ

إِذَا ٱلسَّمَآءُ ٱنشَقَّتْ ﴿١﴾ وَأَذِنَتْ لِرَبِّهَا وَحُقَّتْ ﴿٢﴾ وَإِذَا ٱلْأَرْضُ مُدَّتْ
﴿٣﴾ وَأَلْقَتْ مَا فِيهَا وَتَخَلَّتْ ﴿٤﴾ وَأَذِنَتْ لِرَبِّهَا وَحُقَّتْ ﴿٥﴾ يَٰٓأَيُّهَا
ٱلْإِنسَٰنُ إِنَّكَ كَادِحٌ إِلَىٰ رَبِّكَ كَدْحًا فَمُلَٰقِيهِ ﴿٦﴾ فَأَمَّا مَنْ أُوتِىَ

كِتَٰبَهُۥ بِيَمِينِهِۦ ﴿٧﴾ فَسَوْفَ يُحَاسَبُ حِسَابًا يَسِيرًا ﴿٨﴾ وَيَنقَلِبُ
إِلَىٰٓ أَهْلِهِۦ مَسْرُورًا ﴿٩﴾ وَأَمَّا مَنْ أُوتِىَ كِتَٰبَهُۥ وَرَآءَ ظَهْرِهِۦ ﴿١٠﴾
فَسَوْفَ يَدْعُوا۟ ثُبُورًا ﴿١١﴾ وَيَصْلَىٰ سَعِيرًا ﴿١٢﴾ إِنَّهُۥ كَانَ فِىٓ أَهْلِهِۦ
مَسْرُورًا ﴿١٣﴾ إِنَّهُۥ ظَنَّ أَن لَّن يَحُورَ ﴿١٤﴾ بَلَىٰٓ ۚ إِنَّ رَبَّهُۥ كَانَ بِهِۦ بَصِيرًا
﴿١٥﴾ فَلَآ أُقْسِمُ بِٱلشَّفَقِ ﴿١٦﴾ وَٱلَّيْلِ وَمَا وَسَقَ ﴿١٧﴾ وَٱلْقَمَرِ إِذَا ٱتَّسَقَ
﴿١٨﴾ لَتَرْكَبُنَّ طَبَقًا عَن طَبَقٍ ﴿١٩﴾ فَمَا لَهُمْ لَا يُؤْمِنُونَ ﴿٢٠﴾ وَإِذَا قُرِئَ
عَلَيْهِمُ ٱلْقُرْءَانُ لَا يَسْجُدُونَ ۩ ﴿٢١﴾ بَلِ ٱلَّذِينَ كَفَرُوا۟ يُكَذِّبُونَ
﴿٢٢﴾ وَٱللَّهُ أَعْلَمُ بِمَا يُوعُونَ ﴿٢٣﴾ فَبَشِّرْهُم بِعَذَابٍ أَلِيمٍ ﴿٢٤﴾ إِلَّا ٱلَّذِينَ
ءَامَنُوا۟ وَعَمِلُوا۟ ٱلصَّٰلِحَٰتِ لَهُمْ أَجْرٌ غَيْرُ مَمْنُونٍۭ ﴿٢٥﴾

سُورَةُ البُرُوجِ

بِسْمِ ٱللَّهِ ٱلرَّحْمَٰنِ ٱلرَّحِيمِ

وَٱلسَّمَآءِ ذَاتِ ٱلْبُرُوجِ ﴿١﴾ وَٱلْيَوْمِ ٱلْمَوْعُودِ ﴿٢﴾ وَشَاهِدٍ وَمَشْهُودٍ
﴿٣﴾ قُتِلَ أَصْحَٰبُ ٱلْأُخْدُودِ ﴿٤﴾ ٱلنَّارِ ذَاتِ ٱلْوَقُودِ ﴿٥﴾ إِذْ هُمْ عَلَيْهَا
قُعُودٌ ﴿٦﴾ وَهُمْ عَلَىٰ مَا يَفْعَلُونَ بِٱلْمُؤْمِنِينَ شُهُودٌ ﴿٧﴾ وَمَا نَقَمُوا۟
مِنْهُمْ إِلَّآ أَن يُؤْمِنُوا۟ بِٱللَّهِ ٱلْعَزِيزِ ٱلْحَمِيدِ ﴿٨﴾ ٱلَّذِى لَهُۥ مُلْكُ

ٱلسَّمَٰوَٰتِ وَٱلْأَرْضِ ۚ وَٱللَّهُ عَلَىٰ كُلِّ شَىْءٍ شَهِيدٌ ﴿٩﴾ إِنَّ ٱلَّذِينَ فَتَنُوا۟
ٱلْمُؤْمِنِينَ وَٱلْمُؤْمِنَٰتِ ثُمَّ لَمْ يَتُوبُوا۟ فَلَهُمْ عَذَابُ جَهَنَّمَ وَلَهُمْ
عَذَابُ ٱلْحَرِيقِ ﴿١٠﴾ إِنَّ ٱلَّذِينَ ءَامَنُوا۟ وَعَمِلُوا۟ ٱلصَّٰلِحَٰتِ لَهُمْ
جَنَّٰتٌ تَجْرِى مِن تَحْتِهَا ٱلْأَنْهَٰرُ ۚ ذَٰلِكَ ٱلْفَوْزُ ٱلْكَبِيرُ ﴿١١﴾ إِنَّ بَطْشَ
رَبِّكَ لَشَدِيدٌ ﴿١٢﴾ إِنَّهُۥ هُوَ يُبْدِئُ وَيُعِيدُ ﴿١٣﴾ وَهُوَ ٱلْغَفُورُ ٱلْوَدُودُ
﴿١٤﴾ ذُو ٱلْعَرْشِ ٱلْمَجِيدُ ﴿١٥﴾ فَعَّالٌ لِّمَا يُرِيدُ ﴿١٦﴾ هَلْ أَتَىٰكَ حَدِيثُ
ٱلْجُنُودِ ﴿١٧﴾ فِرْعَوْنَ وَثَمُودَ ﴿١٨﴾ بَلِ ٱلَّذِينَ كَفَرُوا۟ فِى تَكْذِيبٍ ﴿١٩﴾
وَٱللَّهُ مِن وَرَآئِهِم مُّحِيطٌۢ ﴿٢٠﴾ بَلْ هُوَ قُرْءَانٌ مَّجِيدٌ ﴿٢١﴾ فِى لَوْحٍ
مَّحْفُوظٍۭ ﴿٢٢﴾

سُورَةُ الطَّارِق

بِسْمِ ٱللَّهِ ٱلرَّحْمَٰنِ ٱلرَّحِيمِ

وَٱلسَّمَآءِ وَٱلطَّارِقِ ﴿١﴾ وَمَآ أَدْرَىٰكَ مَا ٱلطَّارِقُ ﴿٢﴾ ٱلنَّجْمُ ٱلثَّاقِبُ
﴿٣﴾ إِن كُلُّ نَفْسٍ لَّمَّا عَلَيْهَا حَافِظٌ ﴿٤﴾ فَلْيَنظُرِ ٱلْإِنسَٰنُ مِمَّ خُلِقَ
﴿٥﴾ خُلِقَ مِن مَّآءٍ دَافِقٍ ﴿٦﴾ يَخْرُجُ مِنۢ بَيْنِ ٱلصُّلْبِ وَٱلتَّرَآئِبِ ﴿٧﴾
إِنَّهُۥ عَلَىٰ رَجْعِهِۦ لَقَادِرٌ ﴿٨﴾ يَوْمَ تُبْلَى ٱلسَّرَآئِرُ ﴿٩﴾ فَمَا لَهُۥ مِن قُوَّةٍ

وَلَا نَاصِرٍ ﴿١٠﴾ وَٱلسَّمَآءِ ذَاتِ ٱلرَّجْعِ ﴿١١﴾ وَٱلْأَرْضِ ذَاتِ ٱلصَّدْعِ ﴿١٢﴾
إِنَّهُۥ لَقَوْلٌ فَصْلٌ ﴿١٣﴾ وَمَا هُوَ بِٱلْهَزْلِ ﴿١٤﴾ إِنَّهُمْ يَكِيدُونَ كَيْدًا ﴿١٥﴾
وَأَكِيدُ كَيْدًا ﴿١٦﴾ فَمَهِّلِ ٱلْكَٰفِرِينَ أَمْهِلْهُمْ رُوَيْدًۢا ﴿١٧﴾

سُورَةُ الأعْلى

بِسْمِ ٱللَّهِ ٱلرَّحْمَٰنِ ٱلرَّحِيمِ

سَبِّحِ ٱسْمَ رَبِّكَ ٱلْأَعْلَى ﴿١﴾ ٱلَّذِى خَلَقَ فَسَوَّىٰ ﴿٢﴾ وَٱلَّذِى قَدَّرَ
فَهَدَىٰ ﴿٣﴾ وَٱلَّذِىٓ أَخْرَجَ ٱلْمَرْعَىٰ ﴿٤﴾ فَجَعَلَهُۥ غُثَآءً أَحْوَىٰ ﴿٥﴾
سَنُقْرِئُكَ فَلَا تَنسَىٰٓ ﴿٦﴾ إِلَّا مَا شَآءَ ٱللَّهُۚ إِنَّهُۥ يَعْلَمُ ٱلْجَهْرَ وَمَا
يَخْفَىٰ ﴿٧﴾ وَنُيَسِّرُكَ لِلْيُسْرَىٰ ﴿٨﴾ فَذَكِّرْ إِن نَّفَعَتِ ٱلذِّكْرَىٰ ﴿٩﴾
سَيَذَّكَّرُ مَن يَخْشَىٰ ﴿١٠﴾ وَيَتَجَنَّبُهَا ٱلْأَشْقَى ﴿١١﴾ ٱلَّذِى يَصْلَى ٱلنَّارَ
ٱلْكُبْرَىٰ ﴿١٢﴾ ثُمَّ لَا يَمُوتُ فِيهَا وَلَا يَحْيَىٰ ﴿١٣﴾ قَدْ أَفْلَحَ مَن تَزَكَّىٰ ﴿١٤﴾
وَذَكَرَ ٱسْمَ رَبِّهِۦ فَصَلَّىٰ ﴿١٥﴾ بَلْ تُؤْثِرُونَ ٱلْحَيَوٰةَ ٱلدُّنْيَا ﴿١٦﴾ وَٱلْءَاخِرَةُ
خَيْرٌ وَأَبْقَىٰٓ ﴿١٧﴾ إِنَّ هَٰذَا لَفِى ٱلصُّحُفِ ٱلْأُولَىٰ ﴿١٨﴾ صُحُفِ إِبْرَٰهِيمَ
وَمُوسَىٰ ﴿١٩﴾

References – المَرَاجِع

القُرْآنُ الكرِيم (عربي – إنجليزي)
Translated by: Dr. Muhammad Taqi-ud-Din Al-Hilali and Dr. Muhammad Muhsin Khan. 1417 H.

نصّ القُرآن الكريم كاملاً بالرّسم العثماني كما يوافق مصحف المدينة النّبويّة
من حيث الرّسم وعلامات الوقوف بصيغة الوورد (doc) من موقع الكنوز الدّعويّة - (http://www.koonoz.info/2018/03/quran-word.html)

صَحِيحُ البُخارِي (عربي – إنجليزي)
Saheeh Al-Bukhari, (Arabic, English)
Translated by Dr. Muhammed Muhsin Khan

صَحِيحُ مُسْلِم (عربي – إنجليزي)
Saheeh Muslim, (Arabic, English)
(Hafiz Abu Tahir Zubair, Ed., & Nasiruddin al-Khattab, Trans.)

شَرْحُ رِيَاض الصَّالِحِين (عربي – إنجليزي)
Commentary on the Riyad-us-Saliheen (Arabic, English)
Volume1 and Volume 2
Hafiz Salahuddin Yusuf, Ed., & Dr. Muhammad Amin, Trans

القَول المُفيد على كِتاب التّوحِيد (الجزء الأوّل)
شرح فضيلة الشّيخ محمد بن صالح العثيمين
دار ابن الجوزي. الطّبعة الثّالثة 1418 -1999.

تُحفة الإخوان بأجوبة مُهمّة تتعلّق بِأركان الإسْلام
تأليف الشّيخ عبدالعزيز بن عبدالله بن باز
أشرف على تجميعه وطبعه محمد بن شايع بن عبدالعزيز الشايع
الطّبعة الثّانية 1414 هـ - 1995م

المُغْني لإبن قُدامة

تحقيق د. عبدالله بن عبد المحسن التركي و د. عبدالفتاح محمد الحلو. هجر للطّباعة والنّشر والتّوزيع والاعلان / الطّبعة الثّانية 1412 – 1992

صِفةُ صلاة النّبيّ ﷺ من التّكبير إلى التّسليم كما تراها

تأليف الشّيخ محمد ناصر الدّين الألباني

مكتبة المعارف للنّشر والتّوزيع – الرّياض

الطّبعة الثّالثة للطّبعة الجديدة 1424 هـ - 2004 م

مِنهاجُ المُسلم

تأليف الشّيخ أبوبكر جابر الجزائري

دار السّلام للطّباعة والنّشر والتّوزيع والتّرجمة

زَادُ المِعاد فِي هَدْي خَيْر العِبَاد

تأليف الإمام ابن القيّم الجوزيّة

تحقيق شعيب الأرنؤوط / عبدالقادر الأرنؤوط

مؤسّسة الرّسالة / الطَّبعة الأولى 1435ه – 2014م

الباعث الحثِيث شرح اخْتصار عُلوم الحديث

تأليف الحافظ ابن كثير / مكتبة المعارف للنّشر والتّوزيع – الرّياض / الطّبعة الاولى1417 هـ - 1996م

رَوضة الأنوار في سِيرة النَّبيّ المُختار

تأليف الشّيخ صَفيّ الرّحمن المباركفور/ الطّبعة الرّابعة 1428 هـ

تَهذيبُ سِيرة ابن هِشام

تأليف عبدالسّلام هارون

مؤسّسة الرّسالة / الطّبعة الثّامنة 1401 هـ - 1981 م

مُختصر حياة الصَّحابة

تأليف الشّيخ محمّد يوسف الكاندهلويّ

دار القلم . بيروت- لبنان/ الطّبعة الثّالثة 1412 هـ - 1991م

Index - الفهرس

قَالَ اللهُ تَعَالَى:

(وَمَن يَبْتَغِ غَيْرَ الْإِسْلَامِ دِينًا فَلَن يُقْبَلَ مِنْهُ وَهُوَ فِي الْآخِرَةِ مِنَ الْخَاسِرِينَ) [آلِ عِمْرَان 85]

"Whoever seeks a religion other than Islam (submission to Allah): it will not be accepted from him; and in the Hereafter, he will be among the losers." (3: 85)

الْحَمْدُ لِلَّهِ الَّذِي بِنِعْمَتِهِ تَتِمُّ الصَّالِحَات

"Praise be to Allah, the One who by His blessings and favors, good works are accomplished."

(صَحيحُ الجَامع - رقم 4640)

Issued by the author - صَدَرَ لِلْمُؤلّف

السَّبعُون المُختارَة مِنَ الصَّحِيحَيْن

ISBN: 978-0-692-88142-2

Books can be purchased on amazon
or by contacting the author at
Email: aa.aboasha@gmail.com

Made in the USA
Monee, IL
30 January 2024

52023265R00089